MAKING HIM KNOWN WITHIN THE WALLS

MAKING HIM KNOWN WITHIN THE WALLS

JANE PRATHER HUSS

with
DR DAVID OSTERLUND

Foreword by
JON E. OZMINT

Making Him Known Within the Walls

Copyright © 2025 by Columbia International University

7435 Monticello Rd.
Columbia, SC 29203
www.ciu.edu

Cover and interior layout by Kelly Smith, Tallgrass Media

Scripture quotations taken from the (NASB®) New American Standard Bible®, Copyright © 1960, 1971, 1977, 1995 by The Lockman Foundation. Used by permission. All rights reserved. lockman.org

All rights reserved.

No part of this book may be reproduced in any form or by any electronic or mechanical means including information storage and retrieval systems, without permission in writing from the publisher. The only exception is for short excerpts quoted in a book review.

Paperback ISBN-13: 978-1-939074-14-0

CONTENTS

Foreword	vii
Preface	xi
1. The Background	1
2. The Blueprint	7
3. The Beginning	17
4. The Becoming	27
5. The Brotherhood	43
6. The Battlefield	59
7. The Beacons of Light	75
Afterword	85
Epilogue	89
Notes	103
Acknowledgments	105
About the Authors	107
For more information	109

FOREWORD

When we insist on having an easy path to walk, we miss many of the blessings of walking the path at all.

I can never relate to those who claim to have no regrets. Looking back on every season of my life, there are things I would do differently. My eight years as director of the South Carolina Department of Corrections (SCDC) were no different.

This project was born during one of the most challenging three years of my life. While I did not miss it altogether, I missed too much of the joy that comes with seeing God at work in real and tangible ways. I did get moments of clarity and perspective, seeing glimpses of God's hand at work but, too often, I allowed the unfairness of my circumstances—and they were unfair—to draw my focus away from the remarkable work that was unfolding. Here's why.

I inherited a mess. I was SCDC's fourth director in four years. The man I was replacing was a proven leader and correctional administrator. In his 17 months on the job, he had assessed and made strides toward restoring focus and accountability in an agency that had been rocked by bad outcomes and corruption. But he worked for a Democratic administration in a Republican state and our legislature took a perverse pride in spending as little as possible on corrections. SCDC had become a whipping boy for the legislature, and many wanted to keep it that way.

My first year as director was brutal. Our state's largest budget shortfalls since Reconstruction forced workforce reductions in our agency from over 7,000 employees to under 6,000. At the same time, we faced record inmate population growth, and we were overcrowded, struggling to fund basic services, and triple bunking inmates in hundreds of 80 square foot cells. We were upside down, managing enormous risk. I had too much on my plate. At times, alone with God and my thoughts, I resented it.

When I traveled to Angola Prison in Louisiana in the fall of 2003 to exchange information on agricultural programs and operations, starting an inmate seminary program was not high on my list of priorities. In fact, it was not even on the page. I was looking for ways to improve our farming operations. I knew that if we continued to lose money in agriculture, our legislature would make the shortsighted decision to sell off our farmland for a one-time budget boost, as had happened in other states. We needed to return our farming operations to profitability. We were successful in that regard, but God had another purpose for my trip to Angola.

During those few days, after a quick tour of their inmate seminary program, God planted a vision in my heart and mind. I needed a solid and committed educational partner—one that understood and shared this vision. During the following months, I grew impatient as I struggled to find that partner.

When Columbia International University (CIU) professor Dr. David Osterlund walked out of my office in March of 2004, I shut my door and thanked God for "finally engaging" on the vision He had given me. I called my wife, Luanne, and told her about the meeting. My circumstances were still difficult, but I saw God's hand clearly in sending a man who understood and shared that vision. In spite of my other problems, I was grateful.

I suspect that Dr. Osterlund sensed that I needed him to make this happen. My staff would work with him, but I needed someone who understood and appreciated that serious discipleship and sacrificial service were central to this program. This was neither reentry nor rehabilitation: it went beyond those concepts.

Execution is always hard. Developing the curriculum and running the accreditation gauntlet took longer than any of us expected. My patience was tested, but CIU never wavered. They proved to be a patient and committed partner, fully appreciating and adopting the long-term nature and payoff of this program, even from the beginning.

Looking back, the CIU Prison Initiative was God's project; while I was fortunate to have a role in bringing it to pass, I was not necessary to the equation. I did not foresee God's plan to use these men to assist our staff in dealing with 15,000 new inmates entering the system every year, just as I never anticipated how integral these CIU grads would be to another initiative a few months later: faith and character-based housing units.

I think that is why I find great comfort in the men and women who have been used by God, both in the pages of the Bible and in broader history; God demands that we strive for perfection, but His purposes are never thwarted by our imperfections. He uses our best efforts and our good intentions in spite of our shortcomings and failures. He did so in this instance, and I hope this story, as told by Jane Huss, will be encouraging.

Jon E. Ozmint

PREFACE

I became involved with Columbia International University's (CIU) Prison Initiative in its first year of classes. But I had been involved in prayer for the program earlier than that. Dr. David Osterlund, the first director of the program, has been a good friend of mine for many years. When I became employed in the CIU Registrar's Office in 2005, he was beginning the work on the Prison Initiative and would often drop by my office to talk about how things were going with the project. There were good days and bad days, so I had a good sense of both the joys and the struggles with this huge undertaking.

As a former teacher, I was always interested in this project, and often wished I had extra time to help in some way. A couple of months after the first cohort began their studies, an opportunity presented itself. The men were having problems getting their high school or GED transcripts, which are required for admission to the university. Since they didn't have internet access and no checking accounts to pay the fees, they were at the mercy of their families to order these for them, and many of them no longer had any contact with their family. Here was my opportunity! This was something I could easily do.

My boss was gracious and let me use any "free" time I had at the office to work on acquiring these transcripts, and my position as an assistant registrar enabled me to request the transcripts without revealing that these students were inmates. I love puzzles, and that is just what some of these turned out to be. I often had to figure out what school district the particular school was in, then find out where to request a transcript, and sometimes I had to request several times to finally receive something. For one student, his school had closed, and we could not find where those records were housed. Fortunately, he had a copy of his diploma in his file, and we were able to accept that. I enjoyed playing detective as I tracked these down. Many of the men had graduated 20 or more years ago, so I had to work with district offices to find where those "old" records were now housed.

The added bonus to me was that I now felt a connection to these students. I kept a chart at home of each student by birthdate and would pray for them during their birth month. This helped keep their names before me. I was able to attend a couple of their chapels and so was able to put a face with a name.

But the biggest blessing was when Dr. Osterlund asked me to play piano at the commencement for the first cohort. I've played for a lot of graduations at all levels, kindergarten to postgraduate. I've even played for graduations where my sons walked across the stage. But none are as moving as watching these inmates graduate.

"If any man is in Christ, he is a new creature; the old things have passed away; behold, new things have come." (2 Corinthians 5:17)

I saw this verse lived out repeatedly as I took part in five graduation ceremonies while I worked at CIU. As I sat beside the keyboard during the program, looking at the graduating cohort before me, I would have to remind myself that these gentlemen had once been "bad men." They had each done something bad enough to result in a long prison sentence. But that is not what they were now. They were "new men," being mightily used by God in one of the most difficult mission fields.

And I felt a strong pull that this story needed to be told. What is going on in South Carolina's prisons is almost miraculous. Since these students study at the institution that houses any new male inmate for 30 to 90 days before he is sent to another prison, until the last few years, they had access to every new male inmate at his most vulnerable time. Prison is now very real to him, and he has no contact with family or outsiders during this time. But if he desired, he could request that our student-inmates stop by his cell and pray with him.

"The Spirit of the Lord God is upon me, because the Lord has anointed me to bring good news to the afflicted. He has sent me to bind up the brokenhearted." (Isaiah 61:1)

Jesus quoted this verse and stated that it applied to Him. These student-inmates also live out this verse every day, both while they are students and when they are sent out into the inmate population after they graduate.

This is the story that needs to be told. May you be encouraged as you read about these "missionaries" among "the least of these."

"And the King will answer and say to them, 'Truly I say to you, to the extent that you did it to one of these brothers of

Mine, even the least of them, you did it to Me.'" (Matthew 25:40)

Jane Huss

Note: There are many quotes in this book. You might think too many. However, from the start, the hope was to have at least one quote from each graduate of the program—and there have been 120 as of this writing. But it is better to "hear" a person's thoughts straight from them, rather than having it paraphrased by me.

So, I pray that you will be encouraged by hearing straight from these men the story of their experiences; both the students and those from CIU and the South Carolina Department of Corrections (SCDC). I have read these quotes at least a dozen times, and I am still moved as I read them. May that be the case with you—may you hear their hearts.

Also, the main content of the book was completed in 2017, but not published until 2025. So while any numbers are out of date for "today," the final chapter includes updated numbers as of 2025, as well as updates on some of the programs.

"Remember the prisoners as if chained with them..."
Hebrews 13:3

1

THE BACKGROUND

"Forgetting those things which are behind and reaching forward to those things which are ahead..." (Philippians 3:13)
Carved in stone at Angola Prison's front gate.

WITH MORE THAN 24 state prisons in South Carolina, there are six maximum security prisons, with one of those being the Reception and Evaluation Center for any male prisoner entering the system. These are designed to primarily house violent offenders and those with longer prison sentences, as well as those with behavioral problems.

The state of Louisiana has one such prison: The Louisiana State Penitentiary, also known as Angola Prison. It houses over 5,000 prisoners, all with over 40 years to serve. It has been reported that the average sentence at Angola is 88 years. The only way out for most of the inmates is a pardon or death—either from natural causes or from execution. In fact, 90% will die in Angola, and the prison is prepared for that with hearses and a workshop that makes coffins (Billy Graham's coffin was made here and stored here for years until he passed away in 2018) and graveyards located on the premises.

Angola is the largest prison in the United States, covering 18,000 acres of an old plantation. Sitting at the end of Louisiana Highway 66, it is bordered on three sides by the Mississippi River, and the fourth side by a heavily wooded area with dense undergrowth and venomous snakes. So, there is little hope of escape.

In fact, Angola is a town in Louisiana with houses and streets—but it is within the walls of the Penitentiary and is the home of first responders and their families.

In the late 1960s, Angola gained the nickname "The Bloodiest Prison in the South" because of the number of inmate assaults. It was often called "the worst of the worst." Prisoners formed gangs for protection, and the shorthanded guards could only stand and watch. For a time, "trusty" inmates also served as guards—and even carried guns. Everyone went to bed at night with newspapers or magazines stuffed inside their shirts to hopefully protect them if they should be stabbed during the night.

In the 1970s, prisoners filed *habeas corpus* complaints, that their sentences should not have added to them the threat of having to survive in prison. A federal judge agreed and took over control of Angola. Things did get better, but it was still just a warehouse, holding these prisoners until they died of natural causes or were executed.

But there was a change coming, in the form of a short, stocky man with radical ideas about how to deal with prisoners with no hope. People of that day typically felt the same way about those in prison with long sentences as many do today: Get them off the streets and throw away the key; they are monsters and need to be treated as such.

But not Burl Cain. He had a vision. These men may be in for life, but they need to HAVE a life while incarcerated. A man with no hope is a dangerous man. These men may have committed horrible crimes, but they are still human beings. "Cain knew that the only hope for such a man is moral rehabilitation. He says, 'Moral people are not criminals. That's why moral rehabilitation is the only true rehabilitation.'" [1]

In 1981, Burl Cain became the warden of Dixon Correctional Institution, which is about 30 miles from Angola. It is a medium-security institution that housed about 1,400 inmates at that time. When he told his mother, she said: "You just remember one thing. I raised you right—to know God —and God will hold you accountable one day. If you don't see that those prisoners have a chance to know Him, He will hold you accountable for their souls."[2] Those words have guided Cain ever since.

The Louisiana State Corrections Director, Richard Stalder, saw what Cain was doing in the Dixon facility and asked him to go to Angola and make a difference there. When he came to Angola prison in 1995, his plan for the men was to enable them to live productive and protected lives. Since most are going to spend their life there, he wanted them to understand that Angola is their home. The men do not wear prison uniforms. Most of the housing arrangements are dormitory-style, and he encouraged the men to view their dormitory as a community or a "street"; The man in the next bed is your next-door neighbor—

---

1. Shere, Dennis. 2005. *Cain's Redemption: A Story of Hope and Transformation in America's Bloodiest Prison.* Northfield Publishing. p. 51.
2. Ibid. p. 492.

visit him; keep your "street" free from drugs and stealing; go to church together.

His vision was not to make living at Angola a piece of cake, but to make it tolerable. A place that they CAN live, not just exist for the rest of their lives.

There are many "jobs" that the inmates can do to fill their days; Angola is almost completely self-sufficient and is considered a "working farm." They have gardens that grow vegetables for the kitchen, they raise animals for food, there are tailor shops, woodworking, even hobby shops. Everyone has a job to do. In fact, each year the prison produces as much as four million pounds of vegetable crops, and as of 2010 it had 2,000 head of cattle.

The only guards carrying guns are on the towers on the walls and those guarding the men who work in the fields. These guards are also on horseback, which enables them to keep a closer eye on what is going on. No one else has a gun—if they don't carry a gun, it cannot be taken away and used by an inmate —but they all have a walkie-talkie, so that everyone knows what is going on around the prison at all times.

Not every prisoner bought into Cain's vision. But if a man could not work together with others, he found himself in lockdown in a single cell—for as long as he chose to be non-compliant. That was his choice.

For the vast majority of the men, this is as close to freedom as they will ever be. And they appreciate Cain and his vision. He was no "softy"—he could be as firm as necessary. But he treated them like human beings, and he worked diligently to train them to think of themselves and each other the same way.

Since the men could not leave the prison, one of Cain's visions was to bring in outside groups—both for the sake of the men and to show those on the outside that these are not monsters and that they deserve being treated as humans. He brought in Toastmasters and well-known speakers and performers, and the prison has become famous for their semi-annual rodeo, which also provides a venue for the men to sell the things they have made in the hobby shops.

The rodeo didn't begin under Cain's leadership; the first one was held in 1965. But he expanded it and opened attendance to more people. He encouraged the men to participate and continued to expand the shops that enable the men to make money on the things they have made during the year.

He also worked with New Orleans Baptist Theological Seminary to begin offering a four-year degree program for the inmates. They must have either a high school diploma or a GED and be willing to use their degree for the good of the inmates in Angola. They can earn a degree in pastoral studies, theology, and general studies, and can become inmate ministers, inmate lawyers, or literacy teachers (the average education level of inmates is fifth grade). While the Seminary will admit inmates from any denomination, they teach a Christ-centered curriculum, and students must agree to participate in all classes.

This program has created as much media interest as the rodeo, and possibly more. In the 20+ years this program has been in existence, hundreds of men have graduated and continued living in the population—only now as inmate ministers, inmate lawyers, adjunct faculty for the seminary classes—in effect, missionaries among their fellow inmates. Some have even been sent to other prisons in Louisiana for a two-year stint to help in those prisons. Violence and discipline problems have dramatically decreased. In fact, after the program had been in place for 10 years, its effect on the institution—along with the other constructive activities that Warden Cain had instituted—resulted in a 40% decline in the violence of prisoners on prisoners and violence toward security. Visitors described Angola as a "peaceful" place.

This is the program that captured the attention of the director of the South Carolina Department of Corrections, Jon Ozmint, in late 2003.

2
THE BLUEPRINT

(Photo of Jon Ozmint, speaking at a Prison Initiative graduation)

"God put it into my heart ..." (Nehemiah 7:5a)

THE SOUTH CAROLINA DEPARTMENT OF CORRECTIONS (SCDC) was created in 1960 by then-governor Ernest "Fritz" Hollings, but there had certainly been prisons in existence before then. In 1866, the South Carolina Legislature created the first state-level prison, to house inmates that were currently being housed in county facilities. By the time Governor Hollings created the Department of Corrections, there were four state prisons operating around the state, with an average inmate count of 2,044. As of 2017, the department operated 22 institutions, with an average inmate count of 20,000+, and the director is still appointed by and reports directly to the governor.

During the years 2001-2003, South Carolina saw a significant decline in state revenues, and SCDC saw its budget reduced 21%, which was more than any correctional system in the country. Two institutions were closed, and the staff was cut by over 1,000 employees. Mark Sanford was elected governor of South Carolina in 2002, and the man he asked to become the director of the Department of Corrections was Jon Ozmint, who was only 36 years old, making him the youngest director of corrections in the country at that time.

Ozmint was working for a legal firm in Columbia, South Carolina, where he had just been offered a partnership. But he had quite a resume of prosecutorial work for the state of South Carolina: Former deputy attorney general and chief prosecutor of the State Grand Jury, former general counsel for the South Carolina Department of Labor, Licensing and Regulation, and a former assistant solicitor. And to be honest, he had no desire to accept this position.

For Ozmint and his wife, their faith is a major factor in their lives and their decisions. So, they prayed about this new position, and it was actually his wife who encouraged him that this was a huge mission field. He credits her support as a major factor in his taking this position.

> *"(My wife) and I made this not only our job but our ministry. We gave ourselves to it. If you don't feel like you're leaving something of yourself behind, then you either have no soul or you really didn't go all in. And we went all in. We believe in this agency. We believe in the people who work here. And we believe in the inmates."* [1]

Jan. 1, 2003, saw a new director of the Department of

---

1. Published in the *Charleston Post and Courier*—Dec. 22, 2010

Corrections, Jon Ozmint. Since there had recently been a lot of turnover in that position—four directors in the last five years—he agreed to serve at least four years. And he stepped into the middle of the fiscal year, with a projected budget deficit of $50 million. He had a huge task ahead of him!

By June 30 of that year, he had reduced the deficit to "only" $39 million, and over the next couple of years continued to cut expenses and staff to help whittle that number even lower. In that first year, he had to cut staff from 7,000+ to under 6,000, with almost half of those from headquarters. This was as the inmate population grew from 22,00 to over 23,000. So, a reduced staff and an increase in inmate population meant they had to work smarter, and that meant they needed to go back to the basics.

His personal philosophy is to pay attention to details, and he worked to instill this in his staff, both at headquarters and in each of the prisons. As he visited each facility with the outgoing director, Gary Maynard, he was challenged by Maynard to get out of his office as often as possible and visit the facilities in person. He took this idea to heart, and throughout his eight years as director, he visited at least one facility every week. He made a point to not just visit the day staff, but to also be sure he was an equal presence for the night employees as well, which often meant leaving home at 2:00 a.m. to be there before they went off duty. These were surprise visits—there was no warning, even to the warden—and the staff soon began calling them "Ozmint raids." Originally, he was making sure that even the small details were being covered: He checked under the cafeteria tables, behind and in the dumpsters, the bathrooms and showers, and the mop closets. If all of those were clean, then it was a pretty safe bet that other things were being done correctly.

But he also made time to talk personally with the staff and the inmates, to get their thoughts and insights.

While the "raids" started out as checking to see what needed correcting, it wasn't long before the staff realized what needed to be done, and the visits evolved into a great way to "catch people doing right." And these visits became an encouragement to him as well as to the staff.

As he would visit prisons, he might not remember names, but he would remember faces of those he had dealt with as a prosecutor. In one of his first visits to Perry Correctional, as he and the warden walked across the yard, inmates kept recognizing him and saying, "Mr. Ozmint." The warden finally remarked that walking with him across the yard was like being at a family reunion—"everybody knows you!"

SCDC has a farm system in its prisons, with the goal of raising as much of the food as possible—both to save money and to give the inmates jobs and responsibilities. When Ozmint took over as director, the farm system was losing money. For instance, there was a hog operation that consistently lost money, so Ozmint decided to increase the profitable beef-raising capabilities, and he knew that Angola prison in Louisiana was known for their success in raising beef.

In late 2003, Ozmint visited Angola. When you visit Angola, you will also be shown the seminary program. The first evening he was there, as he was getting ready to go to dinner, he was sitting on the porch of his room in the guest house, looking out over the Mississippi River and the prison campus. He began to think of what the seminary program had done to change the culture at Angola, and began to think about how it might work in South Carolina.

His impression was how different the Angola program was—it was not a program to facilitate the men as they re-enter society. It was a program to help them lose that "inmate" mentality and begin living their lives as men—affecting their environment where they were at that time. Angola has eight prisons within its 18,000 acres, and their seminary graduates may be sent to one of those prisons to work as chaplains, but at that time they did not leave the Angola property.

By contrast, South Carolina had 29 institutions in 2003, with those institutions spread all over the state. It also has paid and volunteer chaplains, who are trained in that work. While Angola houses only those with veritable life sentences, South Carolina doesn't have as many "lifers." In fact, it has been estimated that almost 97% of inmates in SCDC facilities will eventually return to society. So, the model used at Angola would need some changes to make it work in South Carolina.

Would it even work? With all he had going on to try to correct so many issues already, should he be spending any time trying to develop a new program? As he continued to think and pray about it, both while visiting Angola and on his return to Columbia, he came to the decision that "service to God and to others should not be suspended because of circumstances or geography. The mission field of prison is different, but for some it is God's designated place of life and service." He began to develop some principles that he felt would have to govern a program like this to make it work in South Carolina.

- They would always be sent 2-by-2—that's how Jesus sent his disciples out.
- It would not be a re-entry program.
- It would be an accredited degree only.
- To get into the program, they had to be almost a model inmate with outstanding conduct.

- They would give up their prison "rights," and after graduation would be sent to a prison as needed, not necessarily one at the level they had earned.
- They had to have at least eight years to serve on their sentence, so that they would have time to impact the system.
- They would not get to pick their prison industries job after they graduated.

There is nothing more important to an inmate who is living his life right than the things and privileges he earns by his good behavior. Men who came into this program would be giving up those benefits and the rights they had earned to gain them. A Level 3 institution is maximum security; Level 2 is medium security. An inmate can earn the right to be moved to a Level 2 facility and can also earn the right to a particular prison industry job. Those in this program would be giving up both of those rights. Ozmint knew the only way to find men strong enough to make that cultural change would be to make sure from the beginning that they understood the sacrifice they would be making and were willing to make it.

He knew there could be no compromise on these standards. This program had to prove itself, so that a future director, whether he believed in the program or not, could not dispute its benefit to the system, and so would find it difficult to cancel the program. He also felt that, since studies have shown that inmates involved in a serious religious program have lower recidivism rates, the prisons would be more cost-effective if inmates were prepared for successful re-entry into society before they were released. That would give a double benefit: Graduates of this program could influence society within the walls and could influence the economics of SCDC after they were released.

So, where would this program be housed? How would it be "fleshed out?" It made the most sense to house it in Columbia, since that is the middle of the state. And there were a couple of institutions in Columbia that might work. Most wanted it at Broad River Correctional, because it was a newer prison and better designed. Kirkland Correctional (which is on the same property) now had the Reception & Evaluation Center, so it was thought this program would be another "moving part" that would not be to Kirkland's benefit. Also, with the R&E at Kirkland, Kirkland was now overcrowded.

But Ozmint had moved Bernard McKie into the empty warden chair at Kirkland, saw how he had embraced the position, and how he had changed Kirkland for the better. Putting the program at Kirkland was based on what he had seen in McKie, and he knew that he would hold the program to the high standards Ozmint envisioned. When he talked to McKie about it, McKie was willing and determined to make it work.

Bernard McKie began working in corrections in 1976, while still a graduate student. He had served as a warden in several facilities in South Carolina and was the warden of Kirkland for 12 years. His philosophy has always been "If we change one, and keep one from coming back, it will multiply."

He also says often: "You've got a second chance to make a first impression." He is willing to give a person the benefit of the doubt that the first impression was not the person at their best, and he saw the Prison Initiative as an opportunity to do that. He knew there would need to be several changes made to equip the program, but he felt that anything that had to happen would be worth it.

However, he thought the program would fit better at Broad River, and he listed the potential problems in housing it at Kirkland. But he believed in the concept and was ready to be a part of it. He smiles now when he says that "all those problems I said would be happening if it was at Kirkland? Yep, we had them—and I was the person who had to deal with them."

The other major piece of the puzzle was an educational partner: Who would offer the education and degree? Ozmint had been reading the books of Ezra and Nehemiah in the Bible and was struck that these men were given the same news/vision of Jerusalem. But Ezra was burdened for the temple while Nehemiah was compelled to rebuild the wall. He realized that many people might have the same general vision he had for the Prison Initiative, but he needed a partner who had the same specific vision he had—a focus on training the men to live for God within the system, rather than focusing on their re-entry into society. And it needed to be an accredited program, with classes that met every day.

New Orleans Baptist Theological Seminary handled the seminary degree at Angola and were very interested in doing the same thing in South Carolina. They even had an extension site in Atlanta, much closer to South Carolina. But Ozmint never followed through with them.

Ozmint already had a connection with CIU through a good friend of his, Adrian Despres, a CIU board member, and he sensed God leading him to approach CIU about the project. He met several times with CIU leaders, and when he met with Dr. David Osterlund, he had confidence this was a person who could direct and initiate the program.

Now, Ozmint had his own SCDC staff in place to shepherd the program and he had his educational partner and even a director for the program. Most important was that everyone was of the same mind, that when the students graduated, they would be free of that "inmate" mentality and be able to live their lives for God wherever they were.

As Osterlund became familiar with the first cohort of student-inmates, he also saw the biggest obstacle would be changing their mindset. It would be a work in progress. But there were a lot of things to be done before that first cohort could even be assembled.

3
THE BEGINNING

(Photo of Dr. David Osterlund)

"The kingdom will be the Lord's." (Obadiah 21b)

HISTORY HAS SHOWN us that God will always raise up a man (or woman) to accomplish His task, however great or small that task may be. The inception of the Prison Initiative Program at Columbia International University was no different.

Dr. David Osterlund is a white-haired gentleman who turned 80 in 2017. He is soft-spoken and mild-mannered, but he's no push-over. When he senses God's calling for a project, he simply will not accept "no" as an answer. Little did he foresee the extent to which those qualities would be put to the test over the three years it took to bring the Prison Initiative project to fruition.

Doc O, as his friends and colleagues call him, came to CIU

in 1989 from Northwestern College to be the head of the Music Department. In a few years he had transitioned into the role of dean of the Undergraduate School. By late February 2004, his retirement had been announced, and he found himself wondering what he would be doing next. He looked forward to a "fresh new start," and wondered what that might look like: Writing, workshops, travel, missions—there were so many possibilities that he felt he needed to focus and simplify and not spread out too wide. His journal notations at that time show that he planned to spend the summer untangling and disengaging before he embarked on whatever journey the Lord had planned for him.

However, all those plans changed the very next week. He received a message from Dr. Junias Venugopal, the dean of the seminary at CIU, who wanted Dr. Osterlund to attend a meeting with Jon Ozmint, the director of the South Carolina Department of Corrections. New Orleans Baptist Seminary had approached Ozmint about setting up a program in South Carolina similar to the program at Angola prison, but since the South Carolina inmates typically had no college experience, they would not be able to earn a seminary degree. Dr. Venugopal thought the undergraduate dean would be a better fit to work through the issues than the seminary dean. And Dr. Osterlund thought a two-year associate of arts degree would fit best.

Before the meeting, Doc O's devotional reading was from Jonah 1, and his reading from the Oswald Chambers devotional "My Upmost for His Highest" was also significant: "Never consider whether you are of use—ever consider that you are not your own but His."

The original plan was to work toward facilitating the online courses that were already in place rather than teaching the inmate/students "live." At the end of June, Doc O noted in his journal: "I have become taken by the Prison Initiative which I believe will be a 'God thing!' I want to pursue this to see what the Lord would have me do." He had found his direction and his new focus. God's timing, as always, was perfect.

Jon Ozmint was handling the SCDC side, and Doc O had now taken on the task of coordinating with the Department of Corrections and handling the CIU side. In December of that year Doc O visited Kirkland, where it had been decided that the "classes" would take place. He found three adjoining rooms currently being used for storage, of a good size and quite suitable for a classroom, library, and computer lab or office. He noted that it was a very positive visit with affirmation by the prison officials of the possibility of offering this program. He was very encouraged.

Columbia International University began as Columbia Bible School in 1923 in Columbia, South Carolina. It was a dream of a Sunday school teacher and five of her friends, to address the spiritual needs of Columbia's mill workers and their families. After years of prayer, their dream came true.

In 1929, the name was changed to Columbia Bible College and by 1936, graduate-level courses were offered, a forerunner to what is today the CIU Seminary & School of Counseling. In 1960, the school moved from downtown Columbia to its current location north of Columbia, and in 1994, the name was changed to Columbia International University. It consistently ranks as one of the top regional universities in the South by U.S. News & World Report.

While online courses have been offered for many years, truly online degrees were not available until 2013. The school's focus was mostly on resident students. It is truly a unique place, and part of the educational experience is the in-person student contact with faculty and staff. Expanding that concept into a prison environment would be daunting. But Doc O refused to be defeated. He had the support of many individuals, both at SCDC and at CIU, and just when he hit a low point, the Lord would bring encouragement.

It truly is daunting to read all the particulars that had to be worked out before this program could begin. Think of beginning a college. Now think of working through all the restrictions of a maximum-security prison to accomplish this. There was more than just curriculum and faculty, desks, supplies and library needs. Students would have to meet CIU's admissions standards, as well as SCDC's standards for good behavior. What would happen if a student had a discipline problem in the prison? Would he be dismissed from the program? They would follow a strict schedule of courses, so that they were all in the same course at the same time. What would happen if a student failed a course?

CIU also has fairly rigorous student life standards. So, if these men were to truly be CIU students, they would need to meet the same standards. Since some standards had to be adjusted to fit life in prison, the Student Life Department spent a good deal of time working out adaptations to some of the standards to fit the prison scenario. In the end, there wasn't much difference between the main standards:

- Students are encouraged to spend at least 30 minutes a day, five times a week, in prayer and meditation on the Word.
- Students are expected to be active in attending chapel and willing to take significant leadership and helping roles as determined by their chaplain.
- Sunday is to be set aside and observed as distinct

from all other days of the week (as allowed by the circumstance and setting).
- The use of alcohol, tobacco, hallucinogenic drugs and other forms of narcotics (except under medical supervision) is not permitted, nor is any form of gambling.
- Cinema and viewing of television and video recordings are limited to those that do not violate biblical principles of purity and worthiness.

And when you have a college, you must have accreditation. CIU is accredited by three agencies: SACSCOC (The Southern Association of Colleges and Schools Commission on Colleges), ABHE (The Association for Biblical Higher Education—undergrad only), and ATS (The Association of Theological Schools—graduate seminary only). For a school to make a major change requires the accrediting agencies to sign off on that change. ABHE was not a problem, but SACSCOC is a larger organization and has a much more stringent requirement for instituting change. For instance, their "Substantive Change Document" has 64 steps that must be filled out and met, and this alone took much time as it had to be re-written many times before it was submitted. There was even discussion about whether or not it was even necessary. But having the program accredited was absolutely necessary, so this hurdle had to be worked out.

And then there is funding. Always a problem. But particularly in the prison because the entire program would have to be funded by donations. SCDC could not fund a Christian program without constantly fighting the legality of it, so although they could provide a location and help from their end, they could not finance it. The prisoners certainly couldn't pay tuition. Donors would be needed. But how do you compute the costs of such a program? This would become a major hurdle for Dr. Osterlund, even after the program got under way.

It is almost mind-numbing to read through emails and journal notations that refer to financial issues. Dr. Osterlund would think everything was in place for the budget and everyone was on board, and then at the last minute an administrator would say that wouldn't work, and the process would begin again. This happened multiple times.

For example: The program had no money, as no fundraising had begun. But no fundraising could begin until brochures had been printed. And no brochures could be printed without funds. You get the picture. There is an email exchange in Doc O's journal, where a question was asked about what account to use to pay for brochures and posters. His answer says it all: "Until fund-raising brings in giving for the Prison Initiative, there are no funds. We have no department…we have no account." It is an interesting process to try to fundraise without finances to pay for start-up costs.

And no funds meant no letterhead, envelopes, or a secretary to help with anything. Doc O was able to use other secretaries on campus for a while, but it soon became too much of a burden on their schedules. So, another brick was added on to the pile of disappointments and hurdles to overcome.

In 2005, CIU had a new undergraduate dean who strongly supported the new Prison Initiative program, which was a true blessing to Dr. Osterlund. Dr. Pat Blewett would be instrumental in getting this program running, and he describes the process like this:

"This process was like walking three steps forward and then two steps back… but the Lord was good. We continued to make progress. What should have taken months took years…but the

Lord knew what needed to be done and so we learned patience."

The program was presented to the faculty on Feb. 14, 2005, and received overwhelming approval. Now it was time to officially ask for approval from CIU's accrediting agencies.

The plan was for the inmates/students to go through a rigorous evaluation process, first by SCDC and then by CIU. They would then be housed at Kirkland while in the program. After graduation, they would be sent out to other South Carolina prisons, two-by-two, as "missionaries" to their institution.

In 2005, the decision was made to not offer online courses, but to offer all classes on-site, with faculty teaching in person. Everyone involved felt this was a much better scenario, but it added to the details that needed to be finalized, including how much each faculty member would be paid and how his teaching load at CIU would be affected. This is one of the areas where Dr. Blewett was most supportive. It also made the schedule of classes more difficult because, now that there would be a teacher actually teaching on site, the courses had to work around roll call—the "count"—which usually takes place four times each day and typically lasts at least an hour each time. Not an insurmountable task, but it quickly added up to more time being spent to figure out how to flesh it out.

By 2006, it seemed that everything was in order, and the only thing missing was approval from CIU's accrediting agencies. So, the plan was to begin classes that September. However, that approval continued to be a major hurdle. SACSCOC deferred action on the proposal in July, pending three pieces of additional information, and CIU was informed that a deferral would take 30-60 days to review once the additional information was submitted.

They were so close! After much discussion, it was decided to move ahead, trusting that the approval would come in time to begin classes, hopefully in the fall. Jon Ozmint was not opposed to waiting until spring, but expressed confidence that fall could work, if that is the mark CIU wanted to strive to hit.

On July 5, Doc O, Pat Blewett, Andre Melvin and Mike Fiorello drove to Louisiana to visit Angola prison to see it for themselves. They received a tour of the entire facility, including death row, and had the opportunity to interview many involved with the Angola program. They all agreed it was a productive trip.

In late July, the faculty who would be teaching at Kirkland went through two days of security-related training and orientation at the prison, completed all their applications, security clearances, drug testing, and prepared to begin teaching within the next month. After the security training, Dr. Blewett remembers thinking, "Oh Lord, what have we got ourselves into? The prison does not negotiate for hostages! If you get taken, get as low as possible and perhaps you will not be shot!"

Then, on July 31, CIU was informed that SACSCOC had approved the new program! There was much rejoicing, and SCDC was asked to release applications to prisoners as soon as possible. It appeared that the Prison Initiative was finally going to become a reality.

Instead, August brought another hurdle. Dr. Osterlund and Dr. Blewett were informed that, while everyone had thought that the CIU Board of Trustees had authorized the program, it turned out that they had only authorized them to gain SACSCOC approval; the Board still needed to vote on final acceptance of the program before it could be launched, and their next regularly scheduled meetings were not until October. Many discussions and emails followed but work still continued on the details of the program while its actual start was on hold.

Finally, on Wednesday Sept. 6, 2006, Dr. Blewett passed on to Dr. Osterlund the news they had been waiting for: The Executive Committee of the CIU Board had teleconferenced and had approved the implementation of the Kirkland Associate of Arts program. It was actually a go.

But that didn't mean all the details had been worked out. What would be required during the evaluation process was finalized, the class schedules were settled, work began on getting computers hooked up and library books delivered and shelved (and everything those tasks entail when you have to bring them into a maximum-security prison), and the fundraising process was initiated.

Doc O notes in his journal that he considers Nov. 1, 2006, as a red-letter day. There were 54 inmates who applied for enrollment, but the number had to be narrowed to 32. These 32 would be bussed into Broad River Correctional Institution in November or early December for face-to-face interviews (with a team consisting of CIU admissions counselors, faculty, and administrators, and SCDC personnel including a chaplain and a warden), who would determine which 15 men would be members of the first cohort of students.

Doc O was finally able to develop a day-by-day timeline counting down to Jan.15, 2007, when the first course would be offered. All of the hard work, all of the discouragements, all the encouragements, all the prayers—everything had served a purpose, and was coming to fruition. Dr. Osterlund wrote in his journal:

And so, 2006 came to an end—with the uncertainty of how the program would grow and develop—with the uncertainty that all of our planning and prayer was on target—with the uncertainty of whether or not the various groups that had a vested interest would be able to understand, step up, respond, support the program. Yet, we were immensely encouraged by the attitudes and support of the SCDC personnel, of the financial support that had been demonstrated, of the coming together of equipment, books, materials, and men. We entered 2007 awaiting the start of the first cohort.

4
THE BECOMING

"I will give you a new heart and put a new spirit in you; I will remove from you your heart of stone and give you a heart of flesh."
(Ezekiel 36:26)

AND SO, it began.

Choosing the 15 men for the first cohort had turned out to be a more daunting task than anyone had imagined. The 86 applicants had been narrowed by SCDC staff to 53 of the most qualified, and this number was to be whittled down to 15 and two alternates.

Since CIU has a detailed application process, changes had to be made to accommodate these applicants. For example, the applying student needs references. Doc O notes in his journal that the problem was solved by:

- The chaplain screening and approval will serve as the religious reference.
- The Classification Office review and approval will serve as the character reference.
- The SCDC Administrative review and approval will serve as the second reference of character.
- A letter from my office will be entered into their application packet documenting these decisions by these offices.

Dr. Pat Blewett recalls:

"I remember our Associate Warden who helped that process out. He was not confident that this was going to work, but he knew the Director of Corrections wanted the team to give it a good attempt. We were amazed to watch the staff begin to catch a vision and see potential hope for inmates. Truly this was answered prayer as much as finding our first 15 guys."

CIU had a panel of "readers," who studied the applications and the essays and then met and whittled the list down to 32. These 32 were moved to the Broad River facility to be personally interviewed by a panel consisting of Dr. Osterlund, Dr. Blewett, the dean of students, several from the Admissions Office, an assistant warden, and several chaplains from SCDC.

Those interviews were conducted over two long days, beginning at 8:00 a.m., with an hour for an interview, then 30 minutes for interaction among the interviewers. They planned to end by 5:00 p.m., and Dr. Osterlund remembers:

"We found these to be of generally high quality. We also encountered some game-playing. The process continued

through the day and it was a very good day. On Friday we repeated the process. We had effective and consistent questioning with a break for dinner. We began to realize the seriousness of this project and we sense that we are being watched to see if we really follow through. The process was exhausting emotionally and mentally. We talked together at the end of the day and got preliminary choices made as well as expressing sadness over those who didn't make it. Saturday was a day of recovery."

And so, they had their first cohort of 15 inmate students, with two alternates. That proved to be a wise decision, because in mid-December of 2006, before classes had even started, one of the 15 in the first cohort had to be dropped from the program because of "an investigation of some irregularity." So, the first alternate was put in his place.

Jan. 16, 2007 is an historic day—the first day of class! What had, at times, seemed like an impossibility had finally become a reality! Dr. Blewett described it this way:

"This morning at 8:30, 15 inmates now calling themselves CIU students, Dr. Higgins, Dr. Osterlund, and I spent about 20 minutes praying together. We then handed out new Bibles to each student and some textbooks....and at 9:02, Dr. Higgins began our first course at Kirkland Correctional Facility....the course today is Introduction to Evangelism. PTL!"

Doc O remembers:

"Pictures were taken by camera and by the mind's eye that are still clearly etched in memory. Men in 'tans' sitting in rows, anxious and excited. The day beginning with Introduction to

Evangelism, taught by Dr. Rick Higgins, who has the gift of recalling every name—urging all of us to bend our knees in prayer as the class begins."

It was an emotional day for everyone as the men received their textbooks, something they had not opened in years. Before class began on the first day, they read the first Psalm together: *"Blessed is the man who does not walk in the counsel of the wicked..."* Two inmates asked if they could pray. One man knelt. Then another asked, "Could we get on our knees?" Out of a fresh respect for God, the cohort decided to kneel or stand each time they pray. Isaiah 61:1 was also read, providing hope while declaring, *"...He has sent me to bind up the brokenhearted, to proclaim freedom to the captives and release from darkness for the prisoners..."* Dr. Osterlund told the inmates that while they may not get out any time soon, they will find freedom spiritually.

Each student was given a leather-bound Bible purchased by donors. The name of each student was placed in his Bible, and a note was attached stating these Bibles were given through the efforts of the CIU president, Dr. George Murray. On that first day, the Bibles were distributed to the men in the classroom in a ceremony of sorts—calling each man forward and reading his name and awarding the Bibles as if in an award ceremony. Doc O remembers that the men were deeply moved and overjoyed at this unexpected gift. Each cohort has received a similar Bible, each with their name in it, all provided by donors.

The schedule for the men was a chapel at 8:30, then two courses, and study time after lunch to prepare for the next day. They could never be unattended, so mentors were needed to man the library and computer area. These mentors were CIU students and/or staff, who typically worked a shift of four to five hours, and if someone missed their shift, the student-inmates were not able to access the areas they needed for study. So, there were many hands needed to keep this program running smoothly!

The student-inmates were earning the same Associate of Arts degree that was available on the CIU campus, and they would be studying the same courses. The degree consists of courses in Bible, Theology and Ministry: Survey courses in Old and New Testament and in Bible Doctrine, Evangelism & Discipleship, Principles of both Bible Interpretation (Hermeneutics) and Biblical Exegesis & Exposition, Romans, and Progress of Redemption. Progress of Redemption is not a course in the AA degree at CIU, but it was felt to be of such importance to this program that it was added to the schedule.

Your head swimming yet? They also would study basic English courses, including Composition and Research & Literature, Speech, two courses on World History, Math, and Introductions to both Philosophy and Psychology.

And since they could not study the regular Field Education courses involving ministry, three courses were added that also earned certificates: Men's Fraternity, Hospice Training, and Comparative Religions.

As on the main campus, they were usually enrolled in four to five courses in a semester, two on one day and two on another, alternating. There were class sessions in the morning, and then, in the afternoon, they studied and completed assignments. The Associate of Arts degree required 63 semester hours of courses, at least 24 of them in Bible and Theology, and a minimum cumulative GPA of 2.0. For the most part, these were the same professors and the same coursework as studied on the CIU campus, so these men were in for a busy couple of years as they met the academic standards for this AA degree.

A highlight of their week has always been chapel, which

meets on Monday, Wednesday, and Friday mornings. It starts promptly at 8:30 and ends at 8:55, so class can begin promptly at 9:00. Mondays are usually worship chapels, where the men typically talk about their Bible reading and share what God has been teaching them about the particular passage. This chapel has been foundational in developing the bonding of each cohort. Wednesday chapels usually feature a speaker, whether from CIU or an outside speaker. Friday chapels were reserved for SCDC chaplains, exposing them to the program and to the students so that there is already a connection when the men are sent out to other prisons after graduation. Today they are also used for outside speakers.

CIU schedules Prayer Days, when classes are cancelled and prayer events are planned. It was decided early in the Prison Initiative discussions that Kirkland students should also have Prayer Days. While the class schedule is typically kept, time for prayer is extended. And their prayer time often focuses on praying for the students on the main campus. This has helped these students feel more like "real" CIU students. There have been Prayer Days when students on the two campuses exchanged prayer requests with each other, which has become a highlight for both sets of students.

The Prison Initiative students also observe Fall Break and Spring Break. These are times of refreshment on the Kirkland campus, just as they are for the students on the main campus.

Early on, the professors found that Prison Initiative students were hard workers. The men range in age from 20s to 70s. Most were serving sentences of 10 years to life for crimes that included kidnapping to sexual assault to murder. Several of these men never graduated from high school; they earned their GED while incarcerated. And many had never touched a computer or learned to type. But the Lord sent the perfect faculty for these

The Becoming

men, and while there could be gnashing of teeth over assignments, there was also joy over new things learned, and constant thanksgiving for those who were teaching them.

One interesting thing: It soon became apparent that people interpret Scripture differently, based on their upbringing and surroundings. Doc O noted in his journal in February of that first year:

> *"We have started our third week with the men at Kirkland. We had a deeply insightful chapel this morning talking about Hosea: particularly God's promises found throughout and in particular, the comments of Leon, one of our students. He said that when he was incarcerated, he gave permission to his wife to leave if she couldn't wait. This she chose to do. But later, she returned and he is looking for the time when they can be reunited outside the walls. Scripture takes on a whole new meaning through the eyes of these men. Simple sharing of a sequence of Scripture yields many insights... most of them fresh and to the heart!"*

In another chapel, a student described the Easter story as "Jesus on death row."

And they had more issues than just their schoolwork and assignments. Not only were they in class every day, but they lived together as a 15-man cohort, 24 hours a day. The same dorm, the same cafeteria, the same classroom. Stressful, for sure!

Doc O described it this way:

> *"Tensions erupt, and the strain shows—on Kent who has cancer, on Leon who wants his marriage to succeed, on others who are strong leaders who don't see eye to eye on everything. But they are there taking English Literature, and Old*

Testament Survey, and Biblical Discipleship. They're reading the Bible together—and applying what they are learning to the daily challenges of learning, and living together, in a dark and weary land."

And so, they learned patience along with their "book learning."

The CIU professors and workers were also learning new things. Dr. Blewett remembers one day, early in the program, when he was there teaching:

"The guys had gone to lunch, and I stretched out on a table in the library for a little rest. I had not worried about security since we were the only ones using the space, but when I awoke, to two of our guys shaking me, they said, 'Doc, you can't do this to us!' I was a little confused—Do what? 'You cannot take a nap without locking the door for security reasons. You are laying here with keys and your security badge. If something would happen, we would all be in trouble!' Slowly we learned the system, and that first cohort would care for us more than we could ever care for them."

And their thoughts during this time clearly show how they were being stretched:

One commented on the evidence that they were already having a positive input on their environment: "We are staying on what was the loudest and rowdiest floor. Now it is quiet. "

One of the students has developed his own motivation: "Make your time serve you, while you serve time."

Another expressed his concern for a balanced life. When stressed he goes off the edge. He needed to keep calm and was troubled because he showed anger and lashed out. A fellow student prayed with him, and he said that the stress and burden just melted away.

The men saw themselves as a member of a larger group and often encouraged and helped each other with assignments. Those with computer skills or typing skills were always helping those without.

> "Rocco is performing 'tree surgery' on Terry's paper. He has saved his work 5 or 6 times. He is trying to help put the pieces together."

> "What is the most important lesson I have learned so far? Don't shoot the computer. Some of us old fellas are very intimidated by these things."

Many of the SCDC staff were also quick to offer their encouragements and observations of this new program. One of the officers up to count told Doc O:

"Wonderful thing that you are doing." Doc O invited him to read the work of the students. He stated, "The best men we have here."

Another officer noted that it was "a miracle to see all 15 men always showing up for class—and on time."

Doc O noted some of the issues in his Journal:

> "The role of director of the program brought with it many details—professional, non-professional, political, academic: Terrance wanted to change rooms. The men were housed in the A1 Dorm—a side of a double dorm that included 32 beds in 16 rooms. Intended for two men in a dorm room, we had a full complement of men who were placed by prison administration. The men were placed with fellow prisoners even to the

> *point of assigning either the upper or lower bunk—but little or no decisions were made to accommodate ethnicity or age. Not unlike the general prison population, but hoping for better things, our population sometimes found it hard to get along—tensions would arise if one was a snorer, or if one student stayed up late into the night and the other wanted to sleep—or one simply was older and needed to take care of personal functions who might be placed on an upper bunk. There were many and frequent reasons for men who live together to find that friction and abrasiveness is a part of close quarters. We found that one or two of the men were very hard to live with and they had to have their roommate changed 2 or 3 times."*

All of the problems of college students living together in a dorm, added to all of the problems of a prison facility, along with the problems of a wide range of ages and backgrounds, didn't make Doc O's job any easier. But he and the folks at CIU had great help and encouragement along the way. Dr. Blewett put it beautifully in an email to Jon Ozmint early in the spring:

> *"I want to commend the warden and his staff! The entire staff has been incredible to work with! Without their obvious commitment to the vision and gracious instruction, this project would not have gotten off the ground. Truly the executive leadership team at Kirkland and all those who have helped with this project are worthy of commendation. They have represented the state well, and they have represented SCDC well! We consider it an honor and privilege to serve alongside these professionals."*

Director Ozmint spoke at one of the Prison Initiative chapels in late April. Doc O noted: "This was the first time he spoke to the men, some of whom he placed in prison. The men greeted him with respect and interest. They were surprised at the depth of his faith and the soundness of his message." He makes a point to visit every cohort at least once, even now when he is no longer SCDC director, but a private attorney. And his message is always the same:

> *"God is not in heaven, wringing His hands, trying to figure out how in the world you are serving a life sentence. He knew from the foundations that you would be here, and He has a purpose for you here, as long as He leaves you here."*

While everyone had agreed on the "purpose" for this program, God had some ideas of His own. One of those would become evident early in the fall of that year. During that summer, a couple of inmates had escaped from a neighboring facility, and while they were soon apprehended and returned, it had been decided that the men who were in Kirkland's R&E would now be confined nearly 24 hours a day. That meant they were denied weekly religious service attendance. Doc O notes in his journal that he and Dr. Blewett met with two of the chaplains on Sept. 12, to discuss a possibility of the student-inmates providing Bible studies to the new inmates being processed at Kirkland. While Doc O and Dr. Blewett were open to the possibility, they weren't sure how it could fit into the already tight schedule the students were following. But the men of Cohort 1 had ideas about that as well.

Jon Ozmint says, "While we were thinking practically, God was thinking spiritually." The student-inmates had all been through R&E—some of them twice—so they knew how it worked.

Working in those R&E dorms is in many ways harder than

working with the regular prison population. These are new guys who don't know the system, and the staff don't know them. Plus, the staff is constantly bombarded with questions from them. So, the men of the 1st cohort asked if they could go into the R&E blocks a couple of times a week and help the staff by answering the questions. Then, if anyone asked for prayer or asked to talk about spiritual matters, they were there to do that as well.

Doc O and Dr. Blewett quickly saw the advantage this could be for the Prison Initiative and how it could be used to provide Field Education credits for the students. They worked diligently to fit it into the already tight schedule.

On Tuesday, Oct. 2, the men prepared to begin visiting the R&E cells that night. Doc O remembers that there was obvious tension in the room, because no one knew what was going to happen. The plan was for them to go out two-by-two, starting at 6:15 and ending at 8:15.

The next day, the men brought back words of good results, and there were more positive comments received on Thursday. By the middle of October, they were receiving reports that the dorms were becoming calmer after the men had visited, and Doc O noted in his journal:

> "After two weeks of ministry, each man has been going in for a minimum of 2 hours to a maximum of 6 hours on Tuesday, Wednesday and Thursday. They have visited all of Dorm A and I believe Dorm B. During the first week, over 180 men were given evangelistic, pastoral, and discipleship ministry with over 148 prayer requests gathered and 16 salvation decisions. This is amazing! To have an impact on R&E, those guys who were previously not talked with, now a field of 1400 is remarkable."

The Becoming 39

And the comments of the students were so encouraging:

"A Muslim asked what might he do to be saved. He was listening at the edge of his cot."

Tony said, *"The harvest is plentiful. The guys are grasping for something. A wonderful night."*

Terry and Terrance went to six cells and prayed with all. Terrance said that a lot are repeat offenders:

"The ones that he saw last night were in jail for the second time and another for the 5th time. They are saved but they don't have fellowship with other believers. They try to live godly but don't know too much. The devil traps them and they come back here."

"I asked one, 'What made you come back?' and the fellow answered, 'When I put my Bible down.'"

"They were looking out the doors. Bibles open waiting and full of joy already as we approached."

They also reported that they had: *"very good relationships with these youthful offenders in Cell block A, B and C"* because they have had the same kind of life, have done the same things, and they have had to make a change.

Again, they were thinking practically, but God was thinking spiritually.

While the original plan had been for the students to receive ministry skills in other ways, God already had His plan in place:

The men in the Prison Initiative ministering to their peers, knowing the language, the lifestyle, the culture—and having tremendous results. They are effectively ministering to their own unreached people group! After graduating from the Prison Initiative, as alumni, they crossed paths at other prisons with many of those same men they met while visiting them in R&E. They related how much it meant to have someone reach out to them who knew the "ropes," and tell them about the hope that only Jesus gives.

Since there is little opportunity for the Prison Initiative student-inmates to follow-up after sharing the gospel, there is no completely accurate way to verify how many inmates have become Christ followers. But just the number of visits made in one year gives a picture of the enormity of this mission:

From September, 2007 to September, 2008:
R&E inmates visited = 6667
Dedications to Christ = 912
Rededications = 2002

In fact, a member of Cohort 4 applied for that cohort in 2011 specifically because he had been ministered to in R&E two years before by students in Cohort 2:

"In 2009, while I was an R&E inmate, students from Cohort 2 came to my dorm to conduct a Bible study. That night God birthed a vision in my heart for me to attend the CIU Prison Initiative. In response to this calling, I wrote out the vision on paper and prayed over it. Two years to the day of being ministered to by those students, I became a student myself. The CIU

Prison Initiative is making Christ known within the walls." - Ed (Cohort 4)[1]

Ricky from Cohort 1 explains it beautifully:

"This program is more than a program, it is an outreach ministry that reaches into the pit of darkness to train men to be more than Christians, it trains men to become servant-leaders of a mighty God. These men do not just visit this darkness, they were at one point a part of it."

The men in the first cohort had applied for many different reasons, but they all centered around making a difference in their environment and serving the Lord in whatever capacity He might call them:

Terry: *"I wanted to find purpose and significance to an otherwise 'nothingness' existence."*

Billy C.: *"[To learn how] to make a difference wherever I'm at."*

Terrence: *"I had prayed, asking God to clarify His calling on my life, and God answered that prayer and more. Not only did He have me receive a college-level education, He made it clear that my life-long service (not exclusively) is the sick (hospice), young people/gang members, parents, and the forgotten, using His spiritual gift of exhortation."*

---

1. Note: (SCDC policy prohibits use of the full name or picture of any inmate, for several legal reasons. Therefore, this book will use first name and cohort number to refer to a student.)

In December, Doc O met with Director Ozmint and several others and was given the go-ahead to move forward with a second cohort. The plan was to have a cohort in place, ready to begin study when the previous cohort graduated and moved on.

The first Cohort were guinea pigs of a sort: Would this program work? Had they given up their "rights" for nothing? Could they meet the rigorous course requirements? They had another year to finish, and then, hopefully, there would be a second cohort to continue the program and continue being guinea pigs until all the "kinks" had been worked out.

The year 2007 turned out to be an exciting year, and a year of learning—for the student-inmates, for the staff at Kirkland, and for the staff and faculty of the Prison Initiative, who were learning how to walk with one foot in prison and one foot in the "outside" world.

Doc O wrote in his journal:

"And so, we concluded 2007 with the Prison Initiative off to a strong start and with the talk of a second cohort, the possibility of more housing at Kirkland, and the potential future plan for a program for women. This was a year of high significance—and with a feeling of optimism for the future."

5

THE BROTHERHOOD

"Therefore, if any man be in Christ, he is a new creature: Old things are passed away; behold, all things are become new."
(2 Corinthians 5:17)

"My level of self-esteem/self-worth was at an all-time low prior to the inception of the Prison Initiative program. Honestly, I didn't think that God loved me, and even if He did, how could He ever use me on this side of eternity? The CIU Prison Initiative program gave me back my self-esteem/self-worth. I began to learn who I am in Christ, and although I was a broken piece of clay, I was valuable in God's sight. I have been given the courage to speak out and speak loud about the endless love of our Lord and Savior Jesus Christ. I hoped to achieve a better relationship with Jesus Christ, but I first had to understand that God loved me in spite of me. I learned the

powerful forgiveness of God's love, and although my sins are many, I can rest assured of God's love for me." Joseph (Cohort 1)

"It was a blessing for me to be accepted [and] to meet the people, professors, students, and staff of CIU; and to be accepted as a man of God and not seen as a number was an uplifting life-line that I needed." Ricky (Cohort 1)

"Reflecting on the past 16 years of my incarceration, I can see how God has used the many experiences, whether positive or negative, to mold me into the man He desires for me to be. I still don't fully understand what His plan looks like, but it is such an honor to be a part of something so much bigger than myself. Thanks to CIU and the Prison Initiative program…for the first time in my life I believe that God can use the least of these…even me." Joseph (Cohort 1)

WHILE THE PLAN for this program—from man's eyes—was the practical aspect of benefitting the prison system by bringing a positive focus into negative situations, it was refreshing, almost a surprise, to see the immediate benefit to the members of each cohort. While these men were already Christians, and many of them had already been ministering in their facilities, to see them grow and flourish while being trained was almost a miracle. Many of them speak of a particular professor who made his subject "come alive," or a particular chapel speaker or CIU staff member who helped them through a part of their Christian walk. To spend any time with these men is to marvel at God's ability to totally change a human heart—they are certainly no longer the men they were when they were first incarcerated.

"A high point for me was that for two years I was attending college and not in prison. The atmosphere, classroom setting, and professors treated us like students—there was no constant belittling that we were prisoners. The respect we were shown was so refreshing." David (Cohort 2)

"I wanted to walk in the calling on my life, and this program proved to me that I'm right where God wants me to be. I also wanted to learn more about the Bible, and I did!" Timothy (Cohort 3)

"One of the biggest things I learned was to fully trust God when things look hopeless. I have to remember that this work is His, I'm just someone He's using to carry it out." Kelvin (Cohort 3)

"Before CIU, I was unaware of God's purpose for my life. I was defeated by the failures of my past, broken by the pain of my sins, and content with the fate of being unworthy of God's affection. After CIU, I knew that was a lie. I also knew I couldn't hide that truth from those who believed the same lies I once believed myself. Andre Melvin once said, 'We cannot hide who we are. God will always put us on display at the greatest vantage point for all to see so that truth is revealed to all who are in the vicinity.' I am honored to be among His trophies on display in a place where most people believe they can never be found—in prison." Derek (Cohort 3)

"What a blessing to be influenced greatly in Biblical studies (which has caused three major theological shifts in my doctrinal stance so far—all for the positive.) And to be treated

as a person rather than a number, a statistic, or an inmate." Wesley (Cohort 3)

"I can't express enough how much CIU has meant to me. A lot of you already know my testimony. The day I started classes there at Kirkland, I didn't know there were four gospels. I didn't even know what "gospel" meant. I just knew that I had an overwhelming thirst for Jesus. I wanted to know Him more than anything else. Well, I know Him. He's more real to me than this pen in my hand that I'm writing with." Christopher (Cohort 2)

But, as has been stated, many of these men had been out of school for many years, and quite a few had earned a GED while incarcerated. And now they were doing college-level work. For some of them, this was a difficult task, and more than one wasn't sure he would be able to finish.

"The hardest thing for me was the schoolwork, especially the block classes!" Timothy (Cohort 3)

"Some of the schoolwork was very challenging, especially as the semesters progressed. But it stretched us in a very positive way." Jeff (Cohort 3)

"Getting back into the system of student, after 30 years, was a struggle—getting back to the process with deadlines and standards." Ricky (Cohort 2)

"There were no easy rides for us. We were pressed down, pushed beyond, challenged intensely. Weekdays were study—weekends were study—holidays were study. We were fully

equipped. All this by those who loved us and poured their very life into us." Antovis (Cohort 4)

"What I learned from the curriculum was a great blessing, but the high points to me were from a few speakers at chapel who seemed to speak on specific needs I had, and I have been able to share those teachings with many people." Dale (Cohort 4)

"I would have to say that public speaking was the hardest thing for me. One night I packed my bags—I was not going to speak. But I made it through, and today, God has shown me the implications of trusting Him." Dean (Cohort 4)

James (Cohort 4) says that he was so introverted that he was like a turtle that always stays in its shell. In fact, he was so introverted that he didn't even know why he applied to the program, and he was not even accepted at first. So having to speak in class and particularly going to the R&E dorms and sharing his faith was very difficult for him. Now he writes, "I am a roaring tortoise outside of his shell, refusing to see my shell again. I am in love with Jesus, and I want everybody to know. The CIU Prison Initiative Program really changed my life drastically. I never dreamed that I would be following in my father's footsteps as a preacher."

In Doc O's journals is a copy of an email from English Professor Mark Wenger, which shows how deeply the student-inmates were encouraged to go in their thinking, and how every subject was ultimately grounded in God's Word.

Doc O,

Here are the lyrics to the song that evolved during devotion time yesterday. All the lines are iambic meter. I have given it a title, although it could change...

Mark Wenger

God's Delight
A Psalm drawn from the Minor Prophets
A devotional hymn from the men at Kirkland, June 2, 2008

God will work glory, not disgrace	(Nahum 3:5) – [Billy K.]
For those of sincere heart.	(Joel 2:13) – [Melvin]
Correct the errors of your ways	(Zephaniah 3:17) – [John S.]
For Judgment Day draws near.	(Nahum 1:3) – [Billy C.]
God will restore -	(Joel 2:18-19) – [Derek]
Do not gloat at fall of evil ones.	(Obadiah 12) – [Kent]
God will restore -	(Joel 2:24) – [John C.]
And gladly will delight and dance o'er you	(Zephaniah 3:17) – [James]
With singing over you, His own,	
With singing over you who are His own.	

Doc O is a man who never lets the grass grow under his feet, and directing this program was no exception. The beginning of 2008 saw him working to develop a Bible study in Camille Graham, a women's facility. On Feb. 25 of that year the first women's class was held, and Doc O was there. He describes it in his journal:

"I am very pleased with the start of a new program—consisting of one class for about 35 women at Camille. They meet in one of the day rooms at Camille—a spacious place—very workable for the women sitting around tables and directing their attention to Mrs. Blackwell. She is a dynamic

teacher—small in stature but large in command and content. It is a winning combination."

He was also instrumental in arranging for the donation of Bibles for the men to hand out as they ministered to the men in R&E:

"As the men go from cell to cell in their evangelistic efforts, they are regularly asked for Bibles. We found that larger print Bibles in contemporary English was desired. We needed the larger print because of the effect of drugs on the eyes of many of the men—and the use of contemporary English because of the limited reading skills of many who had dropped out of school as a part of behavior leading up to incarceration. I made an aggressive request of the Southern Baptist convention for Bibles—which they positively responded to. Shortly after making this request Bibles were delivered for our use."

And then it was summer, and time to interview candidates for a second cohort to begin in August. Again, Doc O's journal entry explains things much better than I can:

"July 21, 2008—This past year has been intense with the Prison Initiative taking my attention continually every day. We have seen the present men through many challenges and great results—there have been tensions of relationship, theology, church attendance, there have been challenges of black and white perception. There has been the challenge of math and psychology. But the men have been successful and will graduate on December 12th. We have gone through the process of reading applications and holding interviews. It has been a very intense and time-consuming experience for the 10

who interviewed candidates for 2 days. I believe we have made good selections but not without stress and some second thoughts. But now it is time to move the new men in (Wednesday August 20) and hold orientation. It is time to put the cohort together as we prepare to define the role of the present cohort as they mentor the new guys."

And, on Wednesday, Aug. 20, as the fall semester began for CIU, so did the fall semester at Kirkland, this time with two cohorts studying. Another classroom was created in the library, so more than one course could be taught at the same time. The men were also all housed in the same dorm. Now, Cohort A would be in class in the morning while Cohort B was either studying in the new room or in the library/computer room. Then after lunch they would swap.

And while the plan of having two cohorts overlap their time in the program had been prompted by a desire to use resources well, it was soon apparent that there was a bigger benefit. The "old" cohort has become a tremendous help and encouragement to the men of the "new" cohort. Again, God was using man's plans for His greater benefit and glory.

The end of the school year seemed to come in the blink of an eye. Even for those students who struggled academically, it was as though time had been too short. Graduation day was upon them.

Commencement was set for Dec. 12, 2008. Before that date, it was necessary to decide which prison in South Carolina each graduate would be sent to minister. The plan had always been to send them out two-by-two, so there were several meetings held with the chaplains of Level 3 institutions (maximum-security), and Pat Blewett drew up a policy for the graduates, emphasizing that they were to be treated as ministers from the standpoint of allowing anything they were told to be withheld from authorities. In other words, they were not to be used as "snitches" in any of their yards. In his words, "It would seem wise for SCDC to follow the same principles as established by the Geneva 3rd Convention (Part IV, Articles 33, 34, 35, 36, 37) regarding the usage of ministry-related chaplains as confidential informants: to paraphrase, no spiritual guide or chaplain-like person within a prisoner population should be used as a confidential informant and/or spy regarding his peers; they should be seen as ministers."

The decisions on where to send the men weighed heavily on Doc O, as he notes several times in his journal for that year. Meetings had begun in September and continued through the fall, and he felt good about the assignments. However, one of the students refused his assignment on the grounds that, while he had been in the program, he had earned a Level 2 designation, and he now didn't want to go back to Level 3. There were several meetings held, many with the student, and he was reminded of his initial agreement to enter the program: that he would be willing to serve wherever needed. Since he was adamant and would not agree to the assignment, there was no choice but to hold him to the standard that had already been set. He was placed on character probation, which meant he could not take part in the graduation ceremony. On the SCDC side, he was immediately removed from the facility and sent to a Level 2 facility and returned to the general population. His credits were not removed, and the hope and prayer was that he would realize what he had given up and eventually be re-instated into the program and receive his degree. In God's providence, it is wonderful to be able to report that this student worked independently in the facility he was sent to, later received his degree from CIU, and was readmitted as a graduate of the program. But all concerned thought that it had been a necessary "problem" to experience and work through.

It was also interesting to see the honor graduate, John, give up his assignment and fill that vacancy. The refusal of one had opened the door for another to step up.

Graduation is a special time in the life of a student—a time to reflect on who you have become, to be recognized for your hard work and sacrifices, to be honored for this milestone in your life. Early in the program the leaders realized that, even if it could work to have the inmate-students be on the CIU campus and take part in the on-campus commencement, they would have to do so under armed guard and with at least leg shackles on. That would make this time of honor and recognition be, instead, a time of embarrassment and humiliation.

It was decided to hold the Prison Initiative graduation ceremonies at Kirkland. The Kirkland staff and CIU worked diligently to make this a special day for the graduates. They wear caps and gowns, they receive the same diplomas that the main campus students receive, awarded by the CIU president. They march in procession to the music of Pomp and Circumstance. There are speakers and recognition. It truly is a moving experience. Families are present, the next cohort is there watching and imagining themselves as graduates, many chaplains and SCDC staff attend, and there is a reception afterward where the men mingle and speak with those in attendance. While it is SCDC policy to not show faces of the inmates in pictures or video, photos of the men with their family may be kept as a memento of the day. In fact, Sylvester (Cohort 7) remembers watching the commencement ceremony for Cohort 6 as one of the high points of his time at Kirkland, followed closely by his own graduation!

"The highest point was when I graduated, and when they called my name, I danced down the aisle and got my AA degree!" Steven (Cohort 5)

"Graduation was one of the most memorable moments of my life. That sense of accomplishment and brotherhood—priceless!" Jeff (Cohort 3)

The speaker for the first graduation was Warden Burl Cain, from Angola. His plane was late because, as he described it: "I got up this morning at 3:15 and left wet, cold, snowy Angola. Can you believe it? When we got to the airport, for the first time we can recall, the wings of the plane had to be de-iced. The equipment didn't work, and no one knew how to operate it so we could fly to Atlanta. So it is by the grace of God that I am here!"

He arrived just before the ceremony began, but he was such an encouragement to the men. He wisely spent a good bit of his time "warning" them of what life would now be like for them, now that they would be out in the general population again, but he also offered encouragement, because he had seen the same process in so many of his own men at Angola.

He also praised CIU for stepping up to the plate ("because who wants to take a university to prison?"), and the staff and warden at Kirkland, ("because they had to become believers. They had to believe this would work, and they had to have faith in you"). He said all of this was "because God anointed you and anointed them to do this." It was also an encouragement to those in the program when they received word that Warden Cain had refused the honorarium being sent to him, as well as refusing to have his travel expenses reimbursed. And he was so impressed with the idea of sending them out two-by-two, that he implemented that policy at Angola when they began to send graduates to other facilities in Louisiana.

The graduating students also choose a member of their cohort to speak at graduation. John spoke at the first commencement and discussed the many unknowns the students had faced in their journey, calling them a "little thing" compared to the Sovereign God. He also mentioned CIU's motto: "To Know Him and to Make Him Known."

"So many unknowns for one Known," John said. "It is in all these unknowns in life that we are driven to our knees. In this struggle and in this tension, we grow more like Jesus Christ each and every day."

While not the commencement speaker, Doc O made comments about each man and what he saw in them. He remembers: *"This idea of personal comment was a good and sound one—and it has been the starting point of every graduation since the first one. It became a type of fatherly blessing upon the men and was found to be appreciated by the men."* He based it on the "Hall of Faith" in Hebrews 11 which lists each of the "faithful," and notes their triumphs.

That part of the ceremony was very moving for the men, and showed just how much time Doc O had spent around them, learning who they were and their strengths and weaknesses. And it has, truly, become a high point of the graduation ceremonies.

One of the most interesting graduation ceremonies was for Cohort 3, in 2011. Since he was no longer the director of SCDC, Jon Ozmint was invited to be the commencement speaker, which he gladly accepted. However, there was an interesting development. As he describes it:

"When I was chief prosecutor for the state grand jury, there was a man arrested and charged as one of the suppliers for a big cocaine ring. He was not given much of a deal to plead guilty and was the only one to go to trial. I would see him from time to time in my visits to prisons, and imagine my surprise to see him one day in one of the cohorts of the PI! God had gotten ahold of him, and he had turned his life around. He had gone from one of the worst men I had ever known to being one of the best men to go through the program. Since he was in the graduating class when I was to be the commencement speaker, I asked his permission to speak, since his family would be there, and I had prosecuted him."

Permission was granted. It was a moving speech as Ozmint recounted his connection with the graduate.

While the graduates are excited that their formal studies and assignments are over, there is also a bit of sadness. Many developed close relationships with professors, staff, and especially their brothers in their cohort, most of whom they likely will never see again.

When asked what the hardest thing about the program was for Matthew of Cohort 5, he said, "Leaving." That sentiment was echoed by fellow cohort member Braun who said he would miss "separation from those I had bonded with during the two years."

But they never forgot their reasons for being in this program —to go back to the prisons and share the love of Christ with any who would listen; God's messengers to the "men in tan."

"On graduation day I was able to look back on our past two years as a cohort. It was a blessing to see how we all grew and learned from one another. I left CIU as a humbled disciple, willing to love and learn." Travis (Cohort 5)

> "Leaving was the hardest part of the program for me—I loved the academic challenges and the fellowship. Though it was hard to leave, we were ready to take all we had been blessed with to our yards and bless others." Barry (Cohort 6)

Each man has come from a different background, with a different life story, and has seen God impact his life much more than he could have ever imagined. The following are just two examples of the stories that these men have to share:

> "I have been incarcerated since 1995. I have a 60-year sentence and never thought I would have an opportunity like this, getting a college education—let alone one centered on God's Word. The Prison Initiative Program has made more of an impact—on both mine and my family's lives—than I can relate in a few words. I am forever grateful." Edsel (Cohort 7)

Steven (Cohort 5) began his time in prison in Virginia in 1984 with a sentence of 636 years. He was shuffled to Nevada and back to Virginia before being sent to South Carolina, and along the way he became deeply involved in witchcraft. But God had other plans for him. Twice, he had a dream that he was in a Bible study in the woods, and in 2011, while studying in the program, he was reading in Genesis and was struck by the passage of Joseph and Pharoah, where it says that Pharoah's dream was doubled because it was "a thing established by God, and God will shortly bring it to pass." He looked out his window and saw, across the Broad River, the campus of CIU, which looked exactly like it was sitting in the woods.

> "It was the same as my two dreams in 1996 and 2007, and I immediately began to praise the Lord for His work in my life!"

He continues: "We are all products of our past, but we are not prisoners of the past unless we choose to be. I say choose freedom. 2 Corinthians 5:17 reads, 'Therefore if any man be in Christ, he is a new creature: Old things are passed away; behold, all things are become new.' I know that I am in Christ, and I am a changed man, and I will become a productive part of society when released on parole."

Jon Ozmint remembers:

"I remember when I went to the first graduation, I had to speak, since I was the director. And I couldn't keep my eyes dry. And it hit me that God had blessed me in spite of myself. What I did by doing this—kicking and screaming and protesting internally about the timing of it not seeming to be right—I had robbed myself of much of the blessing. Now, looking back, I had missed it. I wanted God to make the path easy for me to walk in order to do it. When we insist on having an easy path to walk, we miss the blessings of walking the path at all."

Doc O wrapped the year up this way in his journal:

"December 31 Journal Essay: The Prison Initiative continues with very strong attention. Graduation/ disbursement of men/ visibility all around the state. We saw the start of the second cohort and the successful graduation of 14 of 15 men. How they fare in their new role is yet to be seen. We have visibility on TV and newspapers and web. We have financial support. We have interest and support of administration—we need to cultivate better conversation and better support between CIU and SCDC. We need to stabilize the curriculum and make

plans for the 3rd cohort and the start of the women's side. I need to redouble my efforts to give the help of a steady and committed and warm person. My life is full and rewarding—with the obligations to church and prison and school."

Graduation. The end, right? Not in this program. It is only the beginning.

6
THE BATTLEFIELD

"...He has sent me to bind up the brokenhearted, to proclaim freedom to the captives and release from darkness for the prisoners..."
(Isaiah 61:1)

"The hardest part of the Program for me was learning how to deal with people. I had lived most of my life alone, behind thick walls I had erected. I avoided conflict as much as possible and was as stubborn as a mule, and I didn't like being around people. I thank God for the brothers He surrounded me with that were persistent and patient. These guys chipped away my walls one chunk at a time. Even when I wanted to stay mad for some reason, they would find a way to melt that coldness away. A true family indeed!" Daniel (Cohort 6)

YES, these men were already Christians, but that didn't mean they had it all together. I don't know a Christian who doesn't struggle with things in their life, and these men are no different. Now add to that the fact that they are incarcerated and all the problems associated with that, and their problems have just magnified. But each of these men feels God's calling upon his life, and, as Ricky (Cohort 2) puts it:

> *"We have been trained for the battlefield, and indeed it is just that—a battlefield. So do not diminish the reality of what we are faced with and know that as we serve on the front lines of Christ's army, we can do all things through Him who strengthens us. We have been prepared for just such a mission."*

They have finished two years of being in the "greenhouse," living with a cohort of fellow believers, studying under godly professors who "don't just impart wisdom and knowledge, but they allow the Holy Spirit to use them and open [our] eyes to many truths." Terry (Cohort 7). But now they must step back into what is their "real world"—a prison yard. Remember, in becoming a member of this program, they gave up their right to have any say in what facility they would be sent. While they accepted this, for some of them it was still a hurdle to overcome in their lives.

> *"I fought tooth and nail not to return back to my old yard, and I cried like a baby when I found out that my assignment was [that facility]. I spent six years there and did not want to have to go back. So, I said there were three things I was not going to do: First, I would not work for the chaplain there, then I would not move into the Character unit, and third, that I would not help run the unit. I learned very quickly not to tell God that I am not going to do something! I have filled all three of those*

positions and have seen plenty of opportunities to minister and let my light shine." James (Cohort 4)

"It is sometimes very hard going to a new yard. We are often stereotyped as 'know-it-alls.' Some chaplain administrations have not been very favorable to us—they have their own workers and see us as trying to 'infiltrate' them." Jerry (Cohort 2)

Chris (Cohort 6) is another graduate who was sent back to his "old" yard:

"People are watching to see if I was the same person I was when I left. Men who I spoke to at Kirkland come up often and tell me that when I spoke at their dorm it made an impact. A lot of seeds have been planted and now it's the cultivating process taking place. So, people are watching to see if what was talked about there is walked out here."

Stacy (Cohort 6) says being sent back to his yard:

"...was both a good thing and a disappointment. A good thing because I have seen many who have come to the Lord while I was gone, and a disappointment because I have seen some who were leaders and teachers who have become comfortable and stopped 'being who they were called to be.' So, this is what I believe has to happen. As men of God and men on a mission, we cannot become comfortable, but we must stay committed."

"I have been struggling with the endless 'nothingness' of daily drudgery. Often wondering, are we really making a difference? Jesus sees even if we cannot." Terry (Cohort 1)

Billy (Cohort 1) was already at Kirkland, which he considered a great yard. By applying to the program, he faced the prospect of being sent to a more difficult yard. But he felt he was ready to go wherever God wanted him to be.

Jason (Cohort 2) found that a struggle for him is that "some people look down on me because I have college experience."

> "The purpose of my duties is to educate and help prepare men to go back into a world that may not accept them. My job is to give them the confidence to stand in the midst of trials and not return to jail. A lot of prayer and meditation is needed for the job I have been chosen to do. This semester has been hard because I find myself struggling over what God wants me to do on this yard. I know that he has me here for a reason, but that reason has not come into focus yet. I've got to tell you that it has not been easy, but with God on my side I can't fail."
> Ralph (Cohort 2)

They see themselves in a battle, and their yards are often a battleground.

> "It is important for us to continue to examine ourselves to know where we are in the faith. We often hear others talk about the devil coming to steal, kill, and destroy, but we don't focus on the fact that the devil desires to also choke the life of God out of us. The sign of the devil choking the life of God out of us can be seen when we don't practice those daily readings, prayers, studies, and fellowship. It is my prayer that the Lord will help us identify those things that are trying to suck the life out of us and cut them off. God desires to bring forth much fruit from our lives. Let us press on in Christ and do those things that are good in His sight." Jerry T. (Cohort 2)

"Brothers, welcome back to prison! I know this period is a time that we couldn't wait for, but when the new wore off the reality of ministry, it is not as glamorous and convenient as we anticipated. But guess what? Jesus is flexing His muscle all over the state, so praise Him that He decided to use regular dudes like us!" Jeremy (Cohort 7)

If you are in Christian ministry, I know you can relate to many of these same issues. A friend of mine often says, "Ministry is messy." So true! But Prison Initiative alumni are seeing so many answered prayers in their yards and in their lives. The Prison Initiative began a newsletter for donors, which they titled "A Way Out of No Way." It soon evolved into an annual "magazine" distributed around SCDC so that all could see what was happening with the Prison Initiative. It includes notes from the graduates on prayer requests, blessings, and anything they would like to share. They often use it as a way to encourage each other. They call this newsletter "Acts 29." The Book of Acts has only 28 chapters, so they see the work they are doing as a "new chapter being written in the SCDC institutions of South Carolina—the activity of the saints being sent out two-by-two." (Doc O in the first edition).

"Brothers, I charge you all before God the Father and our Lord Jesus Christ, 'Set the believer an example in speech, in conduct, in love, in faith, in purity.' This is, in my opinion, what the church needs most behind these walls—to see men of God living out their faith—boldly and unashamedly following Christ in the midst of this prison culture." William (Cohort 4)

"For my brothers who are on less fortunate yards (pertaining to ministry), my word of advice is that you pray to God to

burst open the doors. I truly believe that the favor in Christ we are seeing on this yard in regard to ministry is directly connected to the prayers that were lifted to Him and His faithfulness to answer those prayers." Reggie (Cohort 5)

"*Ministry may not look like it did at Kirkland, in fact it may look like the desert with no opportunities to preach or teach—but God has us here for a purpose. God has us right where He wants us.*" Tim (Cohort 6)

"*I see the following as things to Stop/Reduce/Avoid: Stop allowing my aches and pains to affect my ministry; Stop worrying so much and let God have his way; Stop doubting and trust God more.*" Derek (Cohort 1)

"*Brothers, even though we are restrained by our incarceration, and we live with the uncertainty of the chaos of changes to our physical circumstances in our confinement, I must remind myself that our spiritual situation is greater than our temporal issues.*" Dean (Cohort 4)

They often receive much encouragement. KC (Cohort 7) says:

"*I had a guy who told me, 'Please don't change, don't let this environment change you.' That showed me that someone noticed something different about me and they needed or wanted to see something different in their midst. God has reminded me with the same statement at least three times in my 100 days or so on this yard, so I realize we are an 'aroma of life' to plenty of people. We must be willing to walk in their stench and help loose them.*"

Wes from Cohort 3 had some good advice for all of us:

"I have learned if the grass is not greener once you get on the other side of the fence, you should plant more seeds and pray for rain. So that is what I seek to do here: plant seeds (of the gospel) and pray for rain."

In what kinds of ministries are these men involved?

Many prisons around the country now have faith and character dorms. Director Ozmint initiated them in South Carolina as well. Prison Initiative graduates sometimes lead these dorms, and wardens and chaplains see this as another benefit of the Prison Initiative. While moving into these dorms is voluntary, faith and character dorms are proving that they can take men who are on the margin and turn them into good, respectful, honest inmates. This helps give them the push they need to stay out of trouble. Discipline issues have dropped tremendously in prisons with such dorms. Ozmint says the difference is remarkable. Just walking through a faith-based dorm and then a traditional dorm is eye-opening.

Several of the Prison Initiative graduates have begun programs to fit a need at their particular prison, and as men have been moved around, these programs have also begun in other prisons. One of these is called the Xchange Program, which was created by Thomas (Cohort 4) and Derek (Cohort 3), who were assigned to the same facility. It is based on the Prison Initiative program at Kirkland, but upon completion, "graduates" receive a diploma signed by the chaplain and the associate warden of programs for that prison. It is used as a way to instill godly principles into the lives of the men, encouraging them to utilize talents they were given by God.

"The area I see God using me the most is in Celebrate Recovery. Having a past in addiction and going through pre-release in the past, I can relate to where these men are and the fears they have about staying clean. Then, I'm able to share God's deliverance and power that sustains in our weakness." Adam (Cohort 6)

"We are permitted access to all the wards for evangelizing and discipleship and are in the process of working out a schedule to be permitted into the lock-up unit." Eric (Cohort 5)

"Ministry here is a very challenging thing. I believe that is what I like most about it. I found out that this prison is a testing ground for people who say that they are true to their calling." Ralph (Cohort 2)

"For the Unit 9 guys, the common denominator is their age bracket (under 21). They all need encouragement, mentors, and the examples of authentic men. I recall how impressionable I'd been at 17 coming into the Department of Corrections, so I'm reminded (at 37) to "do everything unto the Lord" (Col. 3:17). Several have grown greatly, and I was blessed to baptize two of my younger brothers in Christ (one of whom I had ministered to at Kirkland R&E)." Ryan (Cohort 6)

There are always unexpected challenges for the Prison Initiative alumni to face. James and Billy C., both from Cohort 1, had to manage for a while without a chaplain. On their second day at their first facility after graduation, their chaplain was killed in an accident. They had been thrown into a lion's den of sorts immediately after graduation.

Melvin, also from Cohort 1 lived for a time in one of the most disobedient dorms on his yard. He spent most of his time teaching, preaching, giving spiritual counsel in the dorm, and building relationships in that environment. His gifts for handling hostile situations and being a peacekeeper were used daily.

And there are personal challenges and heartbreaks.

"My Mom died two months after my CIU graduation. I thank God that she got to see her son as a man of God and graduate before her death—she died proud." Travis (Cohort 5)

"The last 10 months have been a struggle within my life after losing my daughter in a car accident. Then I was faced with making the transition from Kirkland to this yard. Even within these trials I have seen the Lord's hand in it all. I feel the Lord is leading me into a ministry to assist others who grieve the loss of a loved one. I'm going to continue to press on with Christ right by my side and even carrying me at times." Maxwell (Cohort 5)

"My brother was tragically killed in a boating accident while I was a student in the program. It was definitely tough, and I was unsure if I would be able to continue in the program. Like many who face sudden tragedy, I questioned God's 'good' (Romans 8:28) in the wake of my brother's death. It was certainly one of the hardest moments of my life, but God used that for His good—He used it to draw many men to Himself as I shared the testimony of my brother's life, and the importance of not waiting too late to accept Jesus Christ as Lord and Savior. He also taught me to trust Him during my trials because 'the testing of my faith produces endurance (James 1:3).'" Derek (Cohort 3)

While the purpose of prisons is to punish lawbreakers, the desire is also to rehabilitate the prisoners while incarcerated so that when they are released—if they are released—they will become productive citizens who will not be re-incarcerated. Many of the Prison Initiative graduates work in programs helping prisoners to become the men they need to be to live "outside" and to be reconnected to their families.

Several of the prisons now have "Great Dads" and "Malachi Dads" programs: After completing "Malachi" their children will come in for a complete day of fun, games, gifts, and communication with their dad, which will help the dads reconnect with their children.

Broad River Correctional has a Bead Project, which utilizes the blind and the mentally challenged inmates to make necklaces for the children who come on a visit. Each necklace has a powerful card that each father must read to the child, affirming them as they grow into biblical manhood or womanhood.

Daniel from Cohort 6 explains his ministry this way:

"I was assigned to Manning Correctional, and when I got here it was a drastic culture shock, coming from Kirkland. I did not like anything about this place, and the temptation to transfer to somewhere more comfortable and closer to home was constantly ringing in my head. In my resolve, I decided to trust that God has me here for a reason and I decided to bloom where I was planted. Then God spoke! As Kirkland is the institution to receive all inmates in South Carolina, Manning is the pre-release institution where most inmates in South Carolina come to prepare themselves for re-entry into society. From day one at this institution, I've been awarded the opportunity to take part in daily programs designed to prepare men for success once released from prison, and evening programs

where brothers come together to fellowship and study God's Word to better prepare us to walk as light in a darkened world. God has allowed me to proclaim His good news to men as they were coming into prison, and now, as they are going back home. If that is not a purposed plan, then I don't know what is—and I'm honored to be a part of it. God is good, and His love is with His children, no matter where they find themselves."

Dean from Cohort 4 also ministers at Manning, and says:

"I see Manning as a strategic location within the state as the new pre-release institution. Here I recognize an opportunity to impact, equip, and inspire men to accept responsibility for their future, their families' future, and the opportunity to be positive leaders in the communities they are going home to. One of the challenges is the brief amount of time we have to work with them here (90 days). Please pray for us and them."

Ralph (Cohort 2) says:

"The purpose of my duties is to educate and help prepare men to go back into a world that may not accept them. My job is to give them the confidence to stand in the midst of trials and not return to jail. A lot of prayer and meditation is needed for the job I have been chosen to do. This semester has been hard because I find myself struggling over what God wants me to do on this yard. I know that he has me here for a reason, but that reason has not come into focus yet."

Several of the prisons now have the SPICE Program, which is an inmate reentry education program for those who have less than a year before their release date. They typically live in the same unit and attend classes all day during the week. The program includes a supervision component to help provide for seamless transition from the institution to the community upon release. John from Cohort 3 works in this program at his institution and says:

> *"Living among the men in the SPICE program is challenging, but at the same time miraculous because of the propensity for a far-reaching impact and change. The multifaceted paradigm of living among the participants mentoring, teaching, counseling, and eating daily with them affords the opportunity for these men to see precisely what living a godly life and being a man of God really is."*

But it isn't just the "other" inmates who benefit from this Prison Initiative Program. Terrence from Cohort 1 provides a poignant reminder of the changes the program can create in the graduates themselves and in their families:

> *"During my last year at CIU—2008, God gave me a heavy heart for reaching out to young, incarcerated fathers. This heavy heart came as I was leaning hard on the Holy Spirit to keep me patient about reuniting with my son, whom I had never heard from or ever seen up to that point. During the summer of 2010, my prayers were answered: I heard my son's voice for the first time, and he sent me a photo of himself. After that phone call, much letter writing and swapping of photos between us, I saw my son in person for the first time ever on Christmas Day 2014. I hugged him for the first time, telling him, 'I love you and I miss you and I'm so sorry for being absent for the last 14 years.' After repeatedly apologizing and telling him how sorry and regretful I am*

about everything, he responded, 'It's okay Dad, let's focus on now.'"

Ministry is messy. Remember that? And it certainly isn't all glamorous. The infirmary in prison is the full-time job/ministry that John C. (Cohort 1) has been called to. And what does he say are his top five primary responsibilities?

1. Cleaning
2. Serving meals
3. Laundry
4. Hygiene
5. Trash detail

All done with the love of God being shown to everyone around him, ready to share the gospel at every opportunity.

Bennie (Cohort 3) also works in the infirmary at his facility:

"My primary responsibilities include caring for infirmary inmates (physically), keeping the infirmary clean, caring for infirmary inmates (spiritually), assisting the doctors and nurses when needed, protecting myself and making sure my character and the integrity of the infirmary are Godly. I spend most of my time serving sick inmates and serving the Lord."

Preston from Cohort 2 works in the kitchen at his facility, which gives him exposure to the whole population, and he says that one of the most important things in his ministry is being an example to those around him, working with patience and integrity.

Melvin (Cohort 1) was asked, "What are your top five primary responsibilities?" This was his reply:

1. Orientation in classification for new arrivals: help them fill out forms properly for the chapel.
2. Make sure inmates are assigned to proper classes for their spiritual growth process.
3. I help inmate personnel in the reference library to do research for biblical truth and interpretation.
4. Conduct spiritual counseling in the library for guys who seek guidance biblically.
5. Instructor for Teaching and Preaching Class including proper biblical interpretation through the hermeneutical process.

"The success of those around me is my mission; it's my responsibility. God has sharpened my life for the benefit of others, not self!" Derek (Cohort 3)

"This is not a Burger King world; we cannot always have things as we desire to have them, regardless of how noble that desire is. Sometimes we are called to endure hardship (2 Timothy 2:3)." Kent (Cohort 1)

"It is a powerful thing to be able to see the holiness of God in the trenches of incarceration—a power that transforms hopeless spirits into life-giving spirits." Daniel (Cohort 6)

And the problems don't always come from fellow inmates. Although the meetings to assign the first cohort to their facilities had included the chaplains from the Level 3 facilities, Doc O notes that:

"Several years later, we learned that some chaplains and administrators thought that the men who were training would

> *be assuming roles as assistant chaplains, replacing the chaplains presently in service. In some institutions, our graduates were viewed with suspicion, and some resentment—and therefore, they were not put to use in any significant way. No way were our graduates going to supplant the authority of the local chaplain or assistant chaplains. Therefore, some of the men were not welcomed nor given significant duties. They had to earn their place—and for the most part they did."*

Many chaplains and administrators now see the benefits of having these graduates in their yard. They can create curriculum for new classes, teach classes, lead Bible studies and counsel inmates. Charles from Cohort 2 is being used in this way at his facility:

> *"My primary responsibilities include serving as a CBU (Character Based Unit) coordinator/counselor (a 24-hour position), and as an inmate pastoral counselor and worship leader. I spend most of my time counseling men within the CBU and training them to approach life differently by adopting a new mindset. I also minister Biblical truths to hungry men, as well as working on a curriculum for a Biblical training class."*

Reginald (Cohort 3) says that, before being admitted to the Prison Initiative he was ministering, but with an empty toolbox. "But now I've been given the tools I need" for the ministry God has called him to do. While he always struggled with academics, since graduation he has worked in education ministries, and sees himself as one day being an adjunct professor. He says he seriously thought about quitting the program a couple of times but sees now how God taught him perseverance through the process.

It has also been interesting to see more and more the effect of the graduates on the men in R&E. Rod from Cohort 8 was introduced to the Prison Initiative when he was in R&E. Anthony (Cohort 5) talked to him, and Rod still remembers what he said: "To get through you must first go through." That really stuck with him, and he knew he wanted to be in the program. Since he had been out of school for a while, he struggled with academics. But there was an older man in Cohort 7, and Rod would just remind himself that, if that man could do it, so could he.

> *"Prison is a hard place to call home, but as we live here, we must learn to adapt to the customs that surround us. And as we do adapt, we must learn to rely on Christ and the Holy Spirit to lead us in our dealings with the people we come into contact with on a daily basis. Keep your head up and eyes on what is above, and God will finish what He has started in your life. I am living proof."* Robert (Cohort 5)

> *"'To know Him and to make Him known inside of the walls' is our mission statement. It is not dependent on the support/non-support of the administration or chaplaincy in our prospective mission fields. It is not dependent on the housing units in which we live or how often we are or are not locked down. It is dependent on our relationship with the Lord, and our desire to rise up and overcome to fulfill His great mission. We have been prepared for every good work (2 Timothy 2:21). I encourage you to be banner bearers of light, with hymns of praise on your lips, who stand in His strength. Our God is greater than any hardship, danger, or denial."* Edsel (Cohort 7)

7
THE BEACONS OF LIGHT

"You are my servant, I have chosen you and not cast you off; fear not, for I am with you; be not dismayed, for I am your God; I will strengthen you, I will help you, I will uphold you with my righteous right hand." (Isaiah 41:9b-10)

WHAT A JOURNEY these men have been on! I assume that they had not been living for Christ before their incarceration, or else they wouldn't be serving the sentences they were given. They have gone from that "low" point in their lives to either being saved or rededicating their lives to Him and His ministry. Then they were accepted into the Prison Initiative Program and became college students. That was quite a shock to many of them! Then they were sent out to their mission field—to the men in tan behind the walls. Quite a transformation, and only possible by God's power and strength in their lives.

The future. What does it hold for the Prison Initiative and its graduates?

Since this is an ongoing program, the quotes and successes and failures don't end, but this writing must. I will wrap up with activities and changes that have occurred through 2017, to give a sense of the fluidity of God's work in this program.

One of the graduates of Cohort 1 earned a bachelor's degree through correspondence from a college in Georgia, with pen and paper rather than computer. His credits, with a concentration in Psychology, transferred to CIU, which issued him his diploma during the graduation ceremony of Cohort 7. His goal is a masters-level degree in counseling, because "that was my (criminal) background, and there are so many guys in here hurting because of drugs and alcohol that the counseling will help me with ministry." -Billy K.

There have been 120 students in 8 Cohorts, and 9 who have been removed from the program, for various reasons. Some were removed before graduation, some after graduation. At the time of this writing, Cohort 9 is nearing the end of their "student" phase. Two of their members have been removed before graduation, and Cohort 10 has begun their studies. The students are allowed into the R & E dorms on Wednesday and Friday evenings to lead Bible Studies, as well as the other nights to simply visit, answer questions, and offer prayer to those who request it.

In 2008, a program began for women at the Camille Graham Correctional Institution, which is just across a parking lot from Kirkland. It was birthed out of a Bible study of about 35 women. From this beginning, in 2012, an Associate of Arts degree program was initiated, patterned after the program at Kirkland. This one was harder to start, partially because of the restrictions on faculty needing to be female, which made finding acceptable

Bible teachers difficult. But those problems were solved, and two cohorts graduated.

SCDC has only two women's prisons, so sending out 30 graduates to help in those prisons quickly overwhelmed the chaplains who tried to find ministry opportunities for the women. There was also the realization that the women never formed as cohesive a bond with their cohort-mates, leading to problems throughout the academic part of the program. Plus, women typically serve shorter sentences so they would often be released soon after graduation. Consequently, the decision was made to close the women's program and return to the Bible study format. The last graduation ceremony was in 2016. But the 30 female Prison Initiative alumni continue to serve the women of SCDC.

As of 2019, there have been 2 South Carolina Governors, a new warden at Kirkland, a new President at CIU, and a new CIU Arts and Sciences Dean. There is a new director of the program, and as 'old' faculty have passed away, retired, or simply moved on from CIU, new faculty have taken their places. And yet the program keeps going.

In 2012, after struggling with health issues, Doc O stepped down as Prison Initiative director and Dr. Andre Melvin stepped into that role. In many ways he is a lot like Doc O: He is soft-spoken with a quick smile, and he is a man who works through the details. He was very involved in the program from the beginning. But God called him away from CIU to pastor a church just a mile from the campus. In time, he would become the Prison Initiative director, managing both roles. He sees himself as a shepherd to the men in the program, while they are students and after they graduate. He considers the Prison Initiative a form of discipleship that models Christ's training of His disciples: they live together and study together for two years and then are sent out two-by-two to minister.

When addressing the graduates of Cohort 7, he reminded them of their unique advantage of being able to relate to inmates as they minister to them.

"Because you are walking in their shoes, you can relate to the inmates better than we could ever relate to them. That's the goal of this program," Andre told the graduates. "You can reach people that I can never reach."

He also sees himself as a mentor to the Prison Initiative alumni. After the first cohort graduated, Doc O and Andre began visiting them to see how they were doing at their assigned prison and assess what needed to change in the program. Another gentleman who often traveled with them was Chaplain Lloyd Roberts, whose official title was Branch Chief Chaplain. Doc O says that he considers Chaplain Roberts to have been one of the individuals who was indispensable to the program from the beginning. In the early years, he provided the chaplain speakers for chapels, and he was always quick to support the program if any chaplains had concerns.

Chaplain Roberts was in the original planning meetings for the program, and was a strong supporter from the beginning. He saw how the program at Angola had helped that prison and was encouraged to think of the benefits that this program could bring to South Carolina prisons. After retiring in 2014, he noted that what made the Prison Initiative a quality program from the beginning was attention to detail.

God is making that evident in two areas in particular. As the result of a lawsuit that was settled in 2015, SCDC has been working to make major changes in the way the needs of the mentally ill inmates are addressed. One of those changes is a Crisis Stabilization Unit at the Broad River Correctional facility.

When it began in 2016, it was the first of its kind in any state institution in the nation. It is for inmates in crisis who require a

24-hour suicide watch. Previously, it had been handled at each institution with just a couple of cells for such purposes. But the manpower needed to provide this at each facility was not possible, so it was combined at the Broad River facility, and 32 of the Prison Initiative graduates were transferred to Broad River and given training. These men gave up their ministry positions in their yards to instead be used by God in this servant role. They are a sounding board to fellow residents who are in crisis, working alongside the team of officers, nurses, mental health techs, etc., stabilizing the residents so that they are able to return to the general population. And they are seeing success, largely because they can relate to them as fellow inmates.

Antovis (Cohort 4), explains this program:

"A soup made of the ingredients of the last six cohorts—men of every walk of life, of various occupational backgrounds. States and countries from around the globe are represented among these. Men once again tasked with a ministry by God in one of the most unique, most rare manners. Challenging—yes; unpredictable—yes; rewarding—definitely. This program is first among its kind on the state level. We were chosen by God to 'work' in it. We've seen successes in the lives of men in the first month of operation. We are hopeful. We celebrate the lives of each other. We worship as one organism. We are prayerful. We know He has plans to prosper us. We look upward. We look onward. We look inward. In Him."

When over 30 of our graduates were removed from their previous yards and placed at Broad River, it sometimes put a hardship on the graduates remaining. Some saw the number of Prison Initiative graduates in their yard go from four to only one —themselves. But they have simply adapted to the change with increased diligence and reliance on the Lord. James from Cohort 1 encouraged them in an "Acts 29" publication to "not give up, give out, or give in."

In the spring of 2017, two inmates in the dorm housing mentally ill inmates at Kirkland killed four other inmates. Many of the remaining men in the dorm didn't feel comfortable talking to SCDC counselors, and so the door was opened for our students to minister in this dorm. At this time, there is discussion about having at least 2 of our graduates posted to live in the dorm to be able to minister to these inmates. Again, they have a relationship that we could never have, and God is using that in mighty ways.

Another new development in September of 2017 was moving death row from Lieber, in the Lowcountry, to Kirkland. There have been no executions carried out since 2011, and there are currently 37 inmates on death row. Our prayer is that the PI students will eventually be able to visit those on death row, to encourage them and pray with them, if they want.

Character-Based dorms are blossoming at SCDC facilities in South Carolina and having a huge impact. But Prison Initiative graduates are seeing some issues developing that could stretch them in years to come. Derek (Cohort 3) says:

> "It's important to recognize that 'no programs will be offered in character-based units that promote conversion (proselytizing) of inmates toward a particular faith or religious preference or criticize the faith of others.' As a prison missionary of the CIU Prison Initiative Program, it has become increasingly more difficult to walk in a manner worthy of my calling in prison. Christians are very quickly becoming enemies of the state. Stay faithful to the calling for which He has called you and continue Making Him Known Within the Walls."

But God's hand is not just being seen in South Carolina! The Alabama Department of Corrections has also been working toward developing a similar program for their institutions. Their director has spent time with Jon Ozmint, discussing the Program in SC and the challenges he faced in setting it up. They sent a couple of delegates to Kirkland in 2015 to explore what is happening there, and in 2016, two of our PI graduates agreed to be transferred to Alabama and serve their time there to help in beginning a similar program there.

There are also graduates who have been released.

The purpose of the Prison Initiative Program was never to help men in their pursuit of parole. In fact, it would be better for SCDC if the men in the program maxed out their sentences, meaning that SCDC had them for many more years to help in the prison environment. Being a member of the program does not, in and of itself, help with parole considerations. But the work that the man has done, both in his studies and since graduation, reflects his rehabilitation and the possibility of being a good citizen upon release. To this date, 13 of the men have been released, one having maxed out his sentence. Those men have continued their journey, to now be living outside the walls. How has this impacted them, and how have they impacted those around them?

I attended a reunion that is held for these men and women who are now on this side of the fences. What a unique blessing, to hear them share what God has been doing in their lives since their release. Parolees must report once a month, which is later extended to once each year. Two of those in attendance had received the blessing that they no longer have to report at all.

One of our women graduates who was at the reunion, Pam, from the women's Cohort 1, says that "God used the Prison Initiative to teach me patience, kindness, and compassion." She also encouraged Prison Initiative alumni to not be "afraid or embarrassed to tell people you were in prison. It can open so many doors and give so many opportunities to minister to people."

So how are our "released" graduates faring? Quite well. James from Cohort 6 was in prison for 20 years, and when he was released, he thought it would be awesome. He has had many opportunities to minister, but it has been very hard. He relies on the fact that God has a plan. He finds it "so busy out here" because of the many distractions, that it's hard to minister in every place he sees.

Charlie (Cohort 4) served 24 years of a life+20-years sentence, and was released before he finished the course work for his degree. While his goal is to still finish his degree, he is now an assistant pastor in Newberry, South Carolina. Charlie says he "sees God's goodness in every step of my life." He is so thankful for the training he received, especially in psychology, which taught him so much about himself.

> "We are living testimonies to how good God is! We were told, when we began the program, that 'you will never be the same.' How true!! I was 47 years old—too old to start college courses. But God was faithful! We intend to continue the mission of what God wants us to do."

John (Cohort 3) served 20 years. He says that he sees God working on his need to build relationships with people. He was speaking throughout the Southeast, but God showed him that he needed to know his own church family and build relationships, rather than just "drop in and drop out." He has a ministry with homeless, along with ministry to others in his church, spending time with them and getting to know them, and telling them about Jesus.

Jason (Cohort 2) says he served "only" 11 years and was 19 when he went in. Today he is working in a seafood restaurant but says "my profession is not working in a restaurant; my profession is telling others about Christ." His says that while people talk about being in a "season" of life, "You can't choose your season, but you can choose your spirit of what you do during that season."

"Keep your eyes on Jesus. He will never let you down. Though the storms may rage, and all hope might seem lost, God will be with you through it all."

Jerry C. (Cohort 2) served 20 years, going in when he was 16. He took a job working at CIU and completed a Bachelor of Arts degree there, while also serving in evangelism at his church and ministering to seniors.

"We don't often see the connection of things as we're going through our life, but God is always working and sometimes lets us see those connections later."

Melvin (Cohort 1) reminds that "man can do things to help, but it takes the Creator to truly change something." He had worked in logistics for 30 years when he went in and was working in a car wash to survive after he got out. But he was thankful for everything God gave him, and God has ALWAYS been faithful. His daughter was a baby when he went in, and now he is able to be in her life. "If you're going through something, you're supposed to go through it," until God is ready for you to move on. You need to be careful to "stay teachable."

James (Cohort 6) enrolled in the bachelor's program at North Greenville University and became employed as a tutor to two homeschooled children.

It is so encouraging to see that many of them keep in touch with each other regularly and see those relationships as a family. This is not something that they have "moved on" from, it is now a part of who they are. Their pride in where the Lord has brought them is so evident.

I was able to play piano for Cohort 8's graduation in December 2016. It is such a blessing to watch these men celebrate their hard work! This cohort graduated 13 men, and another student, David form Cohort 2, was awarded a bachelor's degree, which he had earned while serving at Kirkland. Cohort 9 was in attendance, and the men of Cohort 10 were ready to begin their studies in January.

The cycle continues, as God calls men to His work, while also calling people to teach and mentor those men. Meanwhile, He calls men and women to give financially to enable the training.

> *"The steadfast love of the Lord never ceases; His mercies never come to an end; they are new every morning; great is Your faithfulness." (Lamentations 3:22)*

AFTERWORD

So, what does it take to start a college program in a prison? Wow! Who knew all the issues involved! This book has not even touched on most of them, although I have tried to give you a sense of the immensity of the task.

In looking at this Prison Initiative, it seems that there are two major things that are vital to the success of such a program. The first, and most obvious one, is that God must be the driving force. He must be leading the charge. The CIU Prison Initiative would never be where it is today if it had merely been man's idea. This was God's idea, in God's time.

The second thing needed may be less clear, but I have seen that it is vital. That is, there must be a person with the passion to do whatever is needed to make the program work. Angola had that in Burl Cain. It was his vision, and he was able to bring that vision to fruition through his unwavering belief that his inmates needed this change of mentality over their surroundings.

But Warden Cain was "only" dealing with his facility, not bringing a change to every facility in Louisiana. South Carolina was blessed to have Jon Ozmint as director of the Department of Corrections. He is a man of detail, and that was needed to take the model from Angola and interpret it in a way that would fit the situations in South Carolina. He is passionate about this program. His involvement continues, just not from an "official" capacity. Creating a program that would work throughout the South Carolina prison system required that the director be totally on board. I have heard of chaplains in other states who have tried to promote something similar. But until/unless they are able to get directors, or even governors, on board, they will only be able to make it work in some of the facilities.

But Ozmint couldn't do this alone, especially long term, because the Department of Corrections director serves at the behest of the governor. Governors change, and with new governors often come changes in department heads. The person who would make the program work had to be so committed that he would be willing to give all his time to it. For as long as it took. And that man was Dr. Osterlund. In my mind, HE is the "human" reason this program looks like it does today. God's timing is perfect. Jon Ozmint and Dr. Osterlund were in their positions at the same time, with the same vision, and with the authority to bring things together.

Long before Cohort 1 began their first day of class, Doc O was at Kirkland almost every day, sometimes ALL day. His journal often notes that he went home exhausted. Even after he was no longer the director, Doc. O was often at the prison several times each week for chapel. From the first day, he showed the men respect by calling them by their last name, "Mr. _____," rather than their first name, as is usually the case in the prison setting. Each cohort said they looked on him as a father-figure.

He grieved with those who either dropped out of the

program themselves or had to be removed from the program. He has rejoiced with members upon hearing good news about their families. He has counseled, calmed, mentored and instructed—whatever was needed to assist the men as both students and ministers.

As I write this in 2017, Doc O recently curtailed his involvement with the Prison Initiative to care for his wife who was suffering with serious medical issues. She passed away in May 2017. But even when he was not at the prison, the program was still in his thoughts and prayers every day.

Today (2019), Doc O lives in his native Minnesota where he has also returned to his love for music and choir directing.

Would this program have succeeded without him? Of course, if it was God's will. But in God's divine providence, it was Doc O's work within the CIU framework that brought this program to fruition. Doc O also helped see the program through the transition from Jon Ozmint as director of SCDC to current director, Bryan Stirling. There were key people withing SCDC who had seen the value of the Prison Initiative, who were willing to make sure it continued.

Will there be problems and difficulties? Of course. Will there be discouragements along with the positives? Of course. As a dear friend once told me, "Ministry is messy." But God's hand has been in this ministry from the beginning, and He continues to be seen every day. Soli deo Gloria!

EPILOGUE
BUT GOD ISN'T FINISHED...

"We give thanks to God always for all of you, making mention of you in our prayers; constantly bearing in mind your work of faith and labor of love and steadfastness of hope in our Lord Jesus Christ in the presence of our God and Father, knowing, brethren beloved by God, His choice of you." (1 Thessalonians 1:2-3)

I BEGAN WRITING this book in 2015, with no idea of whether it would ever be published. In 2019, it was "finished." At least I thought it was. But God wasn't ready for it to be published. In fact, I had come to peace with the fact that it was not going to be published. But in the fall of 2024, God decided the time was right. And so, I wanted to update the five years that have passed.

For many of the graduates of the CIU Prison Initiative, studying doesn't end at commencement. Remember Billy K., the student from the first cohort that I mentioned in Chapter 7? He has since earned that master's degree he desired. In fact, of the

214 graduates of the program as of the end of 2024, 20 men and two women have earned bachelor's degrees, and 13 men are working on a bachelor's degree. Meanwhile, two men and one woman have earned master's degrees, while five more men are currently working on a master's degree.

As I write this in January 2025, Cohort #15 just graduated in December 2024, bringing the total number of Prison Initiative graduates to 214. Cohort #16 continues their studies as #17 just began this month.

At least 50 graduates have served their time and been released, as they continue ministering in Jesus' name outside the walls.

God's hand in this program is evident when you consider it is still going strong even with many leadership changes in state government and at CIU. Since this program began in 2007, there have been:

- 2 SCDC Directors
- 3 South Carolina Governors
- 4 CIU Presidents
- 4 CIU Deans of the College of Arts & Sciences
- 2 Prison Initiative Program Directors

Yes, there have been some changes. The Crisis Stabilization Unit that was at Broad River was mostly moved to Kirkland, and our students were moved to that same dorm. So now our students have access to our graduates who are serving in that Unit. There is still a unit at Broad River, and one of our recent December graduates was sent to the chaplain's office there.

Another change has been that death row was moved from Kirkland, although executions still occur at Kirkland. Legal issues were resolved, and there have been a few executions recently. But since death row is no longer at Kirkland, our students no longer have any access there.

I had written before that the state of Alabama was working toward setting up a similar program. There are several states that have since set up similar programs. In fact, since this Program began, there are several local colleges that are now offering classes leading to degrees for inmates in SCDC, and the directors of those programs meet together regularly to help each other work through any problems.

One of the saddest changes for us is that our students are no longer able to go into the R&E area. This is where every new inmate is sent for 30-60 days before being assigned to a facility. It is a dark place, full of depression where prison becomes a reality. Our students were there to answer the many questions new inmates have about prison life. Prison Initiative students prayed with some of the new inmates at their request. Please join us in praying that our students may be able to return to R&E.

The biggest change happened during COVID. Remember when we were to quarantine ourselves as much as possible? Well, SCDC had to completely shut down their facilities for about eight months. No visitors, of course, and the inmates could not leave their dorms, not even allowed to go outside.

This happened in March of 2020, just as a new cohort began studies that January. The Prison Initiative shut down for an entire year. By the second year the students were able to work via a type of "virtual" classes. Finally, in the third year, regular classes returned with faculty and staff allowed back into the prison to teach and assist the men in person.

The current director, Dr. Andre Melvin, said it was quite hard on the two cohorts during that time. Not only was the quarantine and the year of virtual classes difficult, but some also had family and friends who passed away during that time. So, along with the issues of finally starting up the classes and study routines again, the Prison Initiative staff and faculty also spent extra time with the students to help strengthen them emotionally and spiritually.

But Cohort 12, who finished during COVID, could not have a graduation ceremony, because there was still a limitation on visitors. There is still discussion today on how CIU might be able to hold a commencement for them.

I met with Dr. Melvin recently to get an update on how things have changed over the last five years, and I asked him what he would like to say to all who might read this.

"I continually see God's hands ... His hands have always been on this program. In the highs and lows and challenges, God has always made a way for our program to move forward. Even with all the turnover in leadership changes, God has been in this program. It has been challenging ... every cohort is different. They come in as individuals, and in the two years they are in the program they learn how to love God and love one another. I always tell them that they came here because they wanted a higher education, and they wanted to grow in their love of the Lord—which are good things. But what they don't realize is that, in addition to that, they learn to love one another. And in the two years that they are studying, you see a change in them. They might have known some of their fellow cohort members before, but by the end of the two years they are brothers."

He says he used to tell his congregation that he wished he could lock them up together for two years, because then they would be forced to work things out with each other. He always says he sees this as the closest model to Christ's model—as He called that group of disciples and taught them and watched them for that three years or so they were together. Through that training period, the disciples had to learn to get along with each other as well.

If someone hurts us or angers us, we can just walk away or even change churches. Jesus' disciples and the guys in the Prison Initiative cohorts can't do that. They have to learn how to seek forgiveness and give forgiveness.

Dr. Melvin is still a full-time pastor. Combining that with being a full-time director of a college program is often almost overwhelming. But he is quick to say, "One of the reasons I am still doing this is because I can't think of a greater way to impact the Kingdom of God."

This program HAS made a great impact, both within SCDC and outside of the walls, as our graduates are released and return to "real life." But it has not been possible without a great amount of support, especially from those outside the program. This program is possible only because of the supporters who pray and give financially. If you are one of these, thank you! If not, please start today by praying for all that has to happen to make this program work.

PHOTOS

VOLUME 1, NO 1
APRIL 2008

FROM THE DIRECTOR

March 26, 2008

The men in the Prison Initiative Associate of Arts program study hard and take classes that begin at 9:00 a.m. each morning. But before class, we have a 30 minute chapel time and invite speakers and singers who have something to sing or say.

Today, Rod Lewis, guitarist, CIU faculty member, and great friend of our men at Kirkland came and sang and played and spoke. He had some thoughts about Easter - and talked about Paul in Prison and asked the question, "What does it mean to share in the suffering of Christ?" He sang <u>Were You There</u> and <u>When I Survey the Wondrous Cross</u>. But the song that particularly touched all of us today was one by Amos Lee called

All My Friends
All my friends - live in pain/...got broken hearts/...got broken wings/...know how to live/.. are dear to me/...are the ones I chose.
We'll face the winds,
and break the strongest of trees.
And beckon for the sweet, soft, summer breeze.
All my friends.
(Thanks to Terianne Colangelo (xo_terianne@hotmail.com)

The men regularly pray for their fellow students on the other side of the river at the Monticello Main Campus of CIU.

David Osterlund

In this issue:

From the Director	1
Supporting the Prison Initiative	2
Your Gifts at Work	2
From the Men	3
Reading Recommendations	4
Sound Off!!	4

First volume of the CIU Prison Initiative newsletter "A Way Out of No Way," April, 2008.

VOLUME 1, NO 2
JULY/AUGUST 2008

FROM THE DIRECTOR

We have been busy preparing for the next cohort to begin on August 25. Our student handbook is similar to the one the students receive on the Monticello Road Campus, but there are differences. For example, the inmates must follow the following guidelines that the students on the main campus might find difficult to deal with. We invite you to put yourself in the shoes of the inmate student for a while:

BASIC GUIDELINES TO FOLLOW:

Four Standing Counts
1. 4:45 a.m.   3. 3:00 p.m.
2. 11:00 a.m. 4. 9:00 p.m.

Lockdown Times
12:00 a.m. weeknights
2:00 a.m. weekends and holidays

Sick Call
2:00 a.m. Sign up (awake standing at your door)
6:00 a.m. Report to the annex the same day you sign up.

Cafeteria Meals
Breakfast: at clearing of 4:45 a.m. count
Lunch: 12 noon
Dinner: upon being called

Church Services
Sunday: 8:00 a.m.   Church service
Monday: 6:15-8:15 p.m.   Christians in Action church service
Tuesday: 6:15-8:15 p.m.   Joe Taber Bible study
Thursday: 6:15-8:15 p.m.   Prison Fellowship

CIU Ministry Service
On Tuesday, Wednesday and Thursday nights from 6-8 p.m. CIU students go into the R&E dorms to minister. Everyone must complete a minimum of two hours, with a maximum of six hours per week. Conversations with R&E inmates are limited to ministry times. There is to be no talking or contact with R&E inmates while on the yard.

* * *

Would you like to trade shoes and forgo your freedoms for a life of regimentation, rules, and regulations?

Our men in the Prison Initiative follow all of these rules and many more, spoken and unannounced. Yet they have found freedom in Christ and consistently minister and intently study. They work within the rules—and are succeeding! Please pray for them.

David Osterlund

Second Volume of the Prison Initiative newsletter. Notice all the guidelines the students must follow.

The library specifically for the Prison Initiative at Kirkland. The door on the left leads to the classroom.

The computer lab. The library may be seen through the windows on the left.

On the right from the computer lab is the Prison Initiative library. The glass windows beyond are where the second classroom/study room is located. The windows on the left look out into the main Kirkland library.

Dr. David Osterlund and Dr. Rick Swift, former Dean of Students at CIU, before a graduation ceremony for one of the Prison Initiative cohorts.

Jon Ozmint, speaking at graduation after leaving as Director of SCDC.

Graduating students and faculty and staff gather in the Kirkland library before processing to the graduation site.

Prayer before the graduation. This gives a good view of the Kirkland library and the Prison Initiative facilities.

Walking the line to Graduation.

The heads in the foreground are those in the current cohort – thinking about when they will be the graduates. (Jane Huss is peeking above the keyboard on the left.)

Graduates in the foreground, current cohort upper right.

The excited graduates praising the Lord as we sing together.

The current cohort joins in. Some are also graduates assigned to Kirkland.

This is one of my favorite photos. Everything is done that can be done to make this a special day, as much like a "regular" graduation as possible. But we can never forget that this is, indeed, prison. The correctional facility garb is a reminder that these men have committed crimes worthy of long prison sentences. But God has gripped their hearts and has said they are His to be used to further His kingdom. That is why these graduations are so moving.

This is what it's all about — making Him known within the walls.

NOTES

ACKNOWLEDGMENTS

In working on this book, there are many people whose help has been invaluable. First, Dr. David Osterlund (Doc O), for his journals, his memory, his guidance, and his love of this program. This book would not have been possible without him. Grace Dye, for her time as an assistant to Doc O for many years. Dr. Andre Melvin, the current director, who has graciously met with me several times. Jon Ozmint, for his graciousness in meeting with me and answering questions, as well as Warden Bernard McKie. The graduates who were currently serving the program at Kirkland as I was writing, as well as those who have been released who have so graciously given of their time to talk with me. And Chaplain Roberts, who so graciously took the time to interview with me by phone when I was not able to see him in person.

This has been a labor of love on the part of so many people, who greatly love and support the CIU Prison Initiative. We all give God the glory for His work in so many lives. Soli deo Gloria!

ABOUT THE AUTHORS

Jane Prather Huss

Jane Huss is a graduate of the University of Georgia and has been a music teacher and choir director in Christian schools, a worship leader in several churches and at women's retreats, and retired as an assistant registrar at CIU. She has also played for innumerable graduations, weddings, and funerals. She currently  teaches a women's Bible Study at her church and still occasionally leads worship. She and her husband live in Irmo, SC, and have two sons and six grandchildren.

Dr. David Osterlund

For more than six decades, Dr. David Osterlund has taught all ages of students from kindergarten to seminary doctoral students. He has taught choral and instrumental music in public schools in Minnesota and Wisconsin and developed educational television programs there as well. He and his family spent four years

in Ethiopia teaching at the American School and the Good Shepherd School in Addis Ababa. He has served as Division Chair for music and Fine Arts at the University of Northwestern, St. Paul, as well as Music Chairman and College Dean at Columbia International University. He continues to teach for the Academy of music at the University of Northwestern. St. Paul.

Dr. Osterlund's teaching emphasis has been in Music Education, but also included courses in Ethnomusicology, Conducting, Church Music, Piano, and directing the Northwestern University Band, Bethel-Northwestern orchestra, the Northwestern Women's Choir and the Columbia Ambassador Choir and Grad Singers and College and Community Band.

He has also been active in minister of music roles in churches throughout his career, both in the US and in Ethiopia. Although he is officially retired, he continues to direct choirs and serve in his local church, Family Baptist in North Minneapolis.

FOR MORE INFORMATION

Learn more and donate to help support the Prison Initiative:

https://ciu.edu/advancement/initiatives/prison-initiative/

www.ingramcontent.com/pod-product-compliance
Lightning Source LLC
Chambersburg PA
CBHW060839050426
42453CB00008B/759